SEX, POWER AND PLEASURE

SEX,
POWER
——AND——
PLEASURE

by

Mariana Valverde

new society publishers

Inquiries about requests to republish all or part of the
material contained herein should be addressed to:
New Society Publishers,
4722 Baltimore Avenue,
Philadelphia PA 19143, USA

ISBN:
Hardcover 0-86571-107-0
Paperback 0-86571-108-9

This book was originally published by:
The Women's Press,
204–229 College Street,
Toronto, Ontario M5T 1R4, Canada

Cover design by Mike Holderness

New Society Publishers is a project of the New Society Educational Foundation and a collective of the
Movement for a New Society. New Society Educational Foundation is a nonprofit, tax-exempt public
foundation. Movement for a New Society is a network of small groups and individuals working for
fundamental social change through nonviolent action. To learn more about MNS, write to: Movement for
a New Society, PO Box 1922, Cambridge, MA 02238. Opinions expressed in this book do not necessarily
represent positions of either New Society Educational Foundation or Movement for a New Society.

For Lorna Weir

CONTENTS

ACKNOWLEDGMENTS

EVERY BOOK is a collective product, and this one more than most, being grounded both in the collective theoretical discussions of many feminists and in the day-to-day practical discussions of those around me. I cannot individually thank everyone who has been involved in shaping this book therefore, but at least I want to acknowledge my gratitude to those friends and coworkers without whom this book would never have been conceived, much less written and published.

JANE SPRINGER and LINDA BRISKIN, for devising the idea of this book in the first place and believing that I could do it;

the women at *The Women's Press*, and in particular MAUREEN FITZGERALD and MARLENE KADAR, for thoughtful editing and warm support;

LINA CHARTRAND, MARY NYQUIST and JANICE WILLIAMSON, for good talks and useful references;

my colleagues and students in the Women's Studies Programme at the University of Toronto, for providing a fertile environment;

my parents, JOSE M. VALVERDE and PILAR-HEDY GEFAELL, (who may not like everything they see in this book), for helping me from the start to become a writer;

LIZ BRADY and PAT ELLIOTT, for reading parts of the manuscript and making very insightful comments;

CAROLYN EGAN, for being there and believing in me, and for some good critiques;

and finally LORNA WEIR, for a constant supply of ideas, support and warmth, and, last but not least, for cautioning me against glibness.

TEXT LUST: BY WAY
OF AN INTRODUCTION

SEX, POWER AND PLEASURE. Or, Sex: power and pleasure. Other possible titles for this book were: The politics of sexuality (boringly political, won't sell); Putting sex back on the feminist agenda (awkward, somewhat inaccurate, and besides, we don't just want feminists to read this book); The pleasures and dangers of sex (sounds pornographic and in any case it's been used already); Women's sexuality (too clinical); Desire and power (nice, but too similar to another book); Toward a new sexual politic (has potential, but it sounds academic) . . . .

Since this book is all the potential books just listed and more, it was not easy to come up with a title and a short description for marketing purposes. In the end, the editors and I chose the snappy triadic title *Sex, power and pleasure* because it would indicate that this book tries to cover both the desires and pleasures of sexuality and also the power struggles that take place in and around sex. However, while I was writing it I consistently referred to this book as "the sex book."

Many people were shocked, or at least raised their eyebrows, when they heard me refer to "the sex book." Their shock only helped to reaffirm my belief that there was a need for a feminist reexamination not only of "relationships" and of gender roles but also of sex itself. And yet, I was not interested in discussing the physiology of sex or in presenting recipes for a better sexual life. There were too many books already on the market purporting to do just that, and they did not meet the needs of the people I know who are struggling with sexual dilemmas. What was needed, I thought, was a critical work that would be helpful to women (and men) who were looking not for sexual cookbooks but for analyses to help them think differently and more clearly about the whole subject. Therefore I undertook to write not a how-to-do-it book, but a how-to-think book. In other words, the main object of my investigation was not the physical fact of sex, but the varying ideas and implicit assumptions that most of us have about sex and sexuality.

And yet, this is not just an intellectual project, but rather an analysis based on and oriented toward sexual practice. If separating theory from practice is always hazardous, in the area of sexuality this split can be especially dangerous because, among other reasons, most of the time we are not even aware of the implicitly held theories by which we operate. Thus I have tried to focus on theoretical problems not for their own sake but because they arise out of practice or they shed light on our contradictory feelings. And I emphasize throughout the personal and experiential basis of the conceptual tangle that we have come to call "sexuality."

The English language makes an interesting distinction between "sex" and "sexuality." Sex is what we do in bed (or wherever); sexuality, on the other hand, appears to refer to a whole range of questions as well as to sex. Sex is an activity we engage in for a rather small fraction of our time; sexuality, on the other hand, is an ever-present social issue. Before beginning a discussion of what is involved in erotic exchange, in sex (which is the subject of the first chapter) it might be appropriate to examine how and why sexuality is an area of social, religious, ethical and political concern, not to mention personal anxiety. Then we will use these insights about the social meanings of the term "sexuality" to shed some light on the dilemmas facing anyone who wants to write about it. We will see that contrary to what many people think, talking about sex is not a straightforward matter at all, and this difficulty is not only because of modesty and moral dictates.

In a society which packages both political controversies and intimate personal concerns as individually wrapped "issues," sexuality is an "issue" for many different groups, for very different reasons. Indeed, sexuality is not so much an identifiable issue—like abortion, or childcare—as a catch-all term used by different sectors of society to refer to a multitude of issues which cannot be crammed into a single package.

For many individuals, and women in particular, the term "sexuality" involves personal worries about who we are and what we want. It also refers to ethical concerns about values. Hearing the word can give rise to a whole range of feelings, from pure happiness through mild boredom to extreme pain and humiliation.

For the women's movement as a whole, "sexuality" brings to mind sexual politics: our struggles to equalize relations between men and women, to open up social space for bisexuality and lesbianism, and to try to reshape the social forces which have so far guided our personal and collective sexual development.

For conservatives and traditionally religious people, "sexuality" is a term they would rather not hear. But all the talk about "the family" and "morality," about values and decadence, usually involves defending certain firm views about what sexuality is and how it should be regulated and controlled within a particular family structure.

Sexuality is also a controversial issue in the cultural realm. Most twentieth-century writers and artists agree that frank portrayals of people's sexual lives are an integral part of the artist's task, and this belief helps to distinguish twentieth-century art and literature from those of earlier periods. But there have been disagreements verging on pitched battles about *how* this should be done. What men call "frankness" about sex women have called misogyny and glorification of patriarchy. And after many years of discussions, writers and artists are no closer to articulating a definition of erotic art, or even to agreeing that there is a distinction between art and pornography.

Finally (last but not least!) sexuality is an important area of state activity. The police control prostitution and illegal sexual activity of juveniles, gay men, and other "deviants." Legislators ponder pornography legislation; the courts define what is rape and what is consent; and medical experts and social workers single out and control what they perceive to be pathological or antisocial sexual behaviour.

It would thus seem that most institutions and groups in society are in one way or another involved in defining what sexuality is and what role it should play both in society and in individual development. When we go to a movie we are very likely to get some representation of sexual activity and some implicit sexual values; when we look at an ad, we get overt or subliminal messages that prey on our sexual anxiety to get us to buy things; when we go to church we get sermons about marital fidelity. Even around the dinner table, people often discuss who is going out with whom and who is getting married or divorced, making judgements about what is desirable or what is natural.

And yet, this apparent obsession with sex in no way leads us, as a society, to open and honest discussions to clarify our assumptions and solve our practical problems. When Right To Lifers discuss abortion they do so from the standpoint of a particular view of sex, but they seldom make this view explicit. When feminists talk about pornography they seldom examine their personal assumptions about sex, which largely determine their feelings about pornography. And when policemen and judges punish people for breaking obscenity laws, they cloak themselves in the mantle of "the law" or "public opinion," never having to reveal their own sexual ideology and subject it to scrutiny.

We are constantly thinking and talking about sex; but most of the discussions—and even many of our thoughts—occur indirectly, by way of other topics. One of the main purposes of this book is to tackle the issue of sexuality (or, to be more precise, the issues clustered around the term "sexuality") directly. In order to do so it is necessary to unearth some of the fundamental beliefs, fears and myths that have continued to dominate our discussions but which are seldom examined to see where they originated and whose interests they serve.

Sexuality was first constituted as an object of sociological and medical investigation, and was therefore taken away from the jurisdiction of moralists and theologians, not by feminists but by men. Medical experts such as Havelock Ellis, Richard von Krafft-Ebing, and Sigmund Freud thought they were turning on the light of science to illuminate the previously taboo topic of sexuality; what they did not realize was that they were actually creating and inventing something called human sexuality in the process of investigating it.[1]

Prior to the emergence of the "human sexuality" of the medical experts, nineteenth-century feminists had begun to discuss questions that would later be categorized under "sexual politics"; but this attempt to politicize sex and gender relations was carried out indirectly, by way of discussions of prostitution and the double standard.[2] However, once the male experts began to publish works about sexuality, feminists quickly seized the opportunity to bring forward their own sexual concerns. For instance, birth control pioneer Margaret Sanger, a close friend of sexologist Havelock Ellis, used some of his ideas about validating non-reproductive sexual pleasures in order to legitimize her quest to legalize contraception. And Freud's theories about childhood sexual development and about the need to lift the veil of repression were used, and continue to be used, as the starting point of many feminist discussions about sexual identity, gender formation, and the role of sex in society.

In our own day, the experts continue their research and debate, both at the level of social and psychological theory and in empirical investigations (e.g. Masters and Johnson, Kinsey). But the women's movement is now strong enough to no longer need to justify its discussions of sexuality by putting them in a framework developed by medical and psychiatric experts. Since the later 1960s there has been an ongoing and fairly successful attempt to validate non-expert discourse on sexuality, and to allow ordinary women to look at and discuss their sexual experiences and thoughts with each other as a way of getting to know ourselves and reflecting on the socio-political aspects of sexuality. This politicization of sexuality has been a historic achievement, on par with the original opening up of sexuality as a topic of scientific and theoretical importance.

As long as sexuality was only a topic of scientific concern, the discussions presupposed an expert, usually male, in the position of knowing subject. He stood in contrast to the nameless people—often women, homosexuals, or "deviants"—whose sexuality was made into an object of investigation and classified by someone other than themselves. Even on the rare occasions when women or deviants became their own experts, they tended to distance themselves from their own sexuality and to objectify it, dividing themselves into a thinking subject on the one hand and a pathological creature on the other.[3]

Thus, it is quite an achievement that as women and as non-experts we have managed to open up a discussion of sexuality that is self-reflective and does not presuppose a split between theory and experience, subject and object. We therefore have some of the conditions required for taking some control over the social forces and ideologies that have determined our sexuality. As our understanding of these forces deepens, we are better able to decide what we want to change and how we might begin.

Unfortunately, however, the debate on sexuality has not been one of the success stories of the women's movement. As a movement we have achieved remarkable agreement on issues such as affirmative action, childcare and even abortion; but the mere mention of the word "sex" is more likely to cause anxiety and create suspicion than to generate solidarity and hope for the future.

Without entering into a lengthy discussion about why we have made so little headway since the publication of Kate Millett's *Sexual Politics* in 1969—a discussion of this failure is one of the red threads running through this book—we can here outline how things stand now and take stock of the stalemate.

One position that has become quite popular in recent years among both feminist and non-feminist women is one which I would characterize as "sexual pessimism." From a feminist perspective, this has been elaborated most fully by American anti-pornography writers, notably Andrea Dworkin. The sentiments to which Dworkin appeals are widely felt by large numbers of women in consumer capitalist societies. Some of these sentiments are frustration with the slowness of change in gender relations; revulsion at the commercialization of sex and of women's bodies; anxieties about one's own sexuality; uncertainties about our rights and responsibilities in relationships; and despair over the difficulties of transforming both sexuality and its cultural representations.

Many feminists and women at large have come to feel that sexual liberation is not possible or even desirable for women under the present system, and that the best we can hope for is the relative safety of a private committed relationship. In contrast to the heady days of the late sixties and early seventies, young women today are often pessimistic about both men's commitment to change and their own ability to change. When a student in my Women's Studies class was asked to envision sexuality in an egalitarian society, she replied, "Well, you can't change hundreds of years of conditioning." And, as a sign of the times, most other students nodded in agreement.

Sexual pessimism has come to be a powerful force in the women's movement at the same time that the issue of violence against women has gained prominence. Many of the women who do political or social work around the issues of rape, wife abuse and so on are sexual pessimists, as are many anti-porn activists. It seems to me that some amount of pessimism is an unavoidable response to the newly discovered reality of the *massive* abuse of women and children by men who are otherwise "good citizens and fathers," and who often sincerely believe that they are within their rights in beating or raping women and children. However, in most women this pessimism is checked and balanced by glimpses of a world in which women explore their sexual desires without fear of male abuse, and by the recognition that if male sexual violence is a serious problem, so is female sexual unhappiness and guilt. Unfortunately, some leading feminist theorists have chosen to concentrate on male sexual violence as a single-issue campaign without connecting it to struggles for women's sexual rights. Some have even suggested that sexual violence is due to men's innate biological or mental characteristics. Susan Brownmiller's key study of rape, for instance, states that because men have penises they always have the "potential to rape."[4] This confuses men's social power—which is what gives the penis its threatening meaning—with physiological facts. Physiology does not in itself allow men to perform the complex social act of rape; it is rather a patriarchal social system which permits men to abuse women in various ways including rape. Similarly, Andrea Dworkin's book on pornography repeatedly refers to "male power,"[5] not masculine or patriarchal power, as the source of women's oppression.

If one believes that something inherent in men's physiology or psychology leads them to sexual violence, then pessimism is indeed the only rational response. We might as well give up on heterosexuality and stop trying to transform it. However, knowledge of human history can help us to sketch a different picture, one which is not rose-coloured but is not uniformly bleak. We know, or can find out, that for many thousands of years humankind lived in relatively egalitarian gathering-and-hunting societies, in which there were no inequalities of wealth and in which gender roles, while being usually distinct, were not such as to give men wholesale power over women. We can read historians, especially feminist historians, and see the incredible variety of sexual and family arrangements that have existed in different times and places, and thus gain insights into exactly how and why our particular socio-sexual problems developed. And this we can do without naive optimism but without falling into complete despair. If things have changed so much already, surely they will keep changing, especially if we unite to push certain changes along.

Some recent feminist writings have reacted to the pessimism of Dworkin and company by going to the other extreme and denying the importance of masculine power and other social forces governing our sexuality. These women have fallen into a peculiarly American form of self-delusion which minimizes history and sociology and stresses that "you can do it if you really want." That is, you, as a free individual, can explore your private fantasies and desires and manage your life so as to make them come true. This individualist attitude is usually firmly anti-moralist to the point of being sometimes anti-ethical. It is an attitude that I identify as sexual libertarianism or libertarian individualism.

An example of this libertarian individualism is found in an essay by Muriel Dimen in the recent and acclaimed anthology *Pleasure and Danger*. Dimen argues that feminism has stifled women's sexual desires by insisting on such norms as equality and non-traditional gender roles, and thus creating a new morality of what is politically correct in bed. There is a grain of truth in her critique. Many early feminists did act like vigilantes, and some continue to do so today. But there is nothing to be gained by rejecting, in the name of laissez faire sexual politics, all attempts to use political and ethical reasoning to evaluate sexual practices. Her argument is based on the unsubstantiated claim that "the discovery/creation of sexual pleasure is very much an individual journey."[6]

Sexuality is definitely not individual, partly because all activity other than masturbation directly involves someone else, and partly because all sexual desires are largely socially constructed. It is quite arbitrary to focus on the individual and his/her desires to the exclusion of the social context. Sexuality is also not something that we "have," our personal property that we might choose to "share" with others as we might share a summer cottage. Our sexuality is shaped and even *constituted* by and in the relations that we have with others and with society at large. Sexuality is not a thing at all, but rather a *process* (as I will be arguing at more length in chapter one) and it is definitely not a "natural" thing that would unfold by itself in perfect freedom if there were no social constraints from the state, the church, or feminist vigilantes. Certain physiological drives are necessary in order for us to be sexual, but the bulk of what we call "my sexuality" is created in social interaction. Thus I would argue that the idea of sexuality as a thing that each of us privately owns is a myth generated by our individualistic, consumer society, whereby "free" individuals make contracts to barter or sell their sexuality as well as their worldly goods. It is naive to assume that individually owned desires are and will always be the units by which we measure sexuality.

The point is that both the sexual pessimists and the optimistic libertarians neglect historical and sociological analyses in favour of naturalistic assumptions about what sexuality "really" is. The pessimists emphasize the pervasiveness of male sexual violence, and see male and female sexuality as quite different and even contradictory (e.g. lust as inherently male). Gender is the main, indeed almost the only, category in their analysis, and the gender division is presented as absolute and unchanging. The libertarians on the other hand emphasize individual autonomy, assuming that sexuality is a natural force that has been bottled up and suppressed by social regulation. They are hopeful that once we have thrown off the shackles of sexual superstition, we will be free to carry out our desires. For them gender is not as important, for sexuality inheres in the individual alone.

It is easy to see why proponents of these two views would find it difficult not just to find common ground but even to speak to each other politely. In the United States, the debate among feminists abut sexuality has to a large extent degenerated into a shouting match between these two positions. Alternative views are usually dismissed as being either reducible to one of the two extremes or as fence-sitting, compromise responses.[7]

However a number of feminists in the United States as well as in Britain, Canada and Australia, have begun to develop alternative frameworks that avoid the fallacy of essentialism (i.e. trying to define the "essence" of sexuality or of female sexuality as though it were a natural object) in both its optimist and pessimist varieties. In the United States, Black writer Audre Lorde has written eloquently and insightfully about the need for women to reclaim eroticism as a dynamic source of energy.[8] Her approach is an improvement over those who treat sex as "thing."

Lesbian feminist writer Adrienne Rich has managed to combine a sharp awareness of the impact of male domination on women with evocative descriptions of the creative force of sexual love, specifically love between women.[9] One might note that the framework developed by Rich in the context of an analysis of motherhood could be used in an analysis of sexuality. Her framework makes a useful distinction between the patriarchal *institution* of motherhood (as created by medical and childrearing experts and by economic and social forces), and the manifold *experiences* of being a mother and/or daughter. This distinction could be very useful in discussions of sexuality, preventing blanket generalizations such as "sex is good for women" or "sex is male-defined and thus bad for women."

The approach taken in this book makes use of Rich's distinction to overcome some of the stalemates in current feminist debates on sexuality. By stressing that the *institutions* of sexuality—ranging from sexology through pornography to Christian sexual ethics—are particularly oppressive for women because of the male bias in definitions of sexual pleasure, we can see ourselves as the more or less willing objects of the historical and social construction of sexuality. But by simultaneously emphasizing the variety of our own sexual *experiences*, we can try to highlight the ways in which we resist these social forces, counteract them, and sometimes even manage to change them.

Our bodies and our lives are not hopelessly determined by patriarchal oppression—but neither are they capable of complete individual autonomy. We need an approach which does not presuppose a rigid opposition between necessity and freedom, but rather sees sexuality as an open terrain in which the powers of the state, of the scientific and moral establishments, and of the sexist ideology of male-defined pleasure are constantly meeting *resistance* from individuals and groups. The experiences of such individuals and groups give them a starting point to challenge the ideas and power of those who have created the oppressive institutions. As philosopher Michel Foucault has pointed out, the exercise of power, in the sexual as well as in the political realm, always generates both some acquiescence and some resistance on the part of those who are the objects of that exercise. The point is to maximize the resistance and minimize the acquiescence, while being aware of the powers over us.

This dialectical approach sees us both as subjects and objects and regards sexuality as both institutional and experiential. It has been used by some recent feminist participants in the "sex debate," for instance by many of the contributors to both the British feminist anthology *Sex and Love: New Thoughts on Old Contradictions* and the Canadian anthology *Women Against Censorship*.[10] And this is the approach followed in this book, an approach which relies heavily on other discussions but which tries to explore the theoretical issues underlying the current debate in a more thorough and systematic manner than is possible in a single anthology article.

Any attempt to analyze sexuality from a woman-centred, non-expert perspective does not merely require new ideas but, what is perhaps more difficult, a new way of writing. Science and experience have hitherto spoken in different languages, and in order to combine theory and practice our own analysis requires a critical look at both these languages.

Women have for a long time been excluded from the realm of theory, of capital-K Knowledge; and in taking up the tools of theory we have to decide to what extent and in what sense they are appropriate to women thinkers analyzing women's sexual experiences and desires. This is being done in various ways, for instance by women discussing to what extent theoretical frameworks developed by male thinkers such as Freud, Jacques Lacan or Michel Foucault are useful for women thinking about women. The jury is still out on this question, and undoubtedly there will be no single verdict on the relevance of these theoreticians to women-centred thought on sexuality. We will probably integrate some concepts outright, adapt a few others, and reject some—while continuing to disagree among ourselves about the complex question of the relation of feminist thought to non-feminist frameworks for sexuality. However, be that as it may, there is a self-consciousness among feminists about using particular theories, concepts and jargons when discussing sexuality. Women writers tend to be explicitly cautious in their choice of theoretical language.

The other main genre used by women to talk about sexuality is the confessional. It has in contrast been characterized by a remarkable absence of self-consciousness and methodological reflection. We seem to believe that we can just "tell" our sexual story, forgetting that perhaps in the "telling" we are also constructing our experience. The experience we have constructed fits into a particular model of a story—the "true confessions" model, for example, the pornographic model, or the Christian confessional mode. We have all read novels, watched soap operas, and been influenced by the various codes and conventions regulating what constitutes an interesting or realistic story. We also have a sense of the need to fit into a particular moral framework when telling a story about sex. Sex stories are usually either uplifting (that is, finishing with a conversion and clear moral for the reader) or they are exhibitionistic and pornographic. And in recounting our most intimate experiences and feelings we naturally use the literary and moral conventions available to us, without reflecting on how these might affect our perception of what is important or even of what actually happened.

Several of the assumptions underlying our attempts at sexual truth-telling are readily apparent. We seem to operate on the presupposition that telling one's sexual story is therapeutic for the writer; educational and/or uplifting for others, if only by letting them know that their problems are not unique; and useful to feminism as a whole, insofar as our own stories—be they comedies, tragedies, or melodramas—are building blocks for what is often referred to as "women's experience."

A typical and widely read example of women's sexual confessional literature, which will be used here to analyze the theoretical assumptions just listed, is Kate Millett's *Sita*,[11] an autobiographical account of the feminist writer's obsessive-compulsive love affair with another woman. Interestingly, the lesbian component of this account is not that important, and heterosexual reviewers, including many men, stated that they completely identified with Millett's tale of tragic love. It is a characteristic of confessional literature that the social context of the experience is minimized, and what is brought to the foreground is the private dialectic of joy and sorrow, fulfilment and despair, with which everyone can easily identify.

Whether or not writing the book was therapeutic for Millett as author, the reader is clearly not in a position to tell. But we can state that Kate as protagonist appears to be remarkably unchanged by both the experience of the love affair and of its writing (she informs us that the writing began while she was in the midst of the affair). At the end of the book she is indeed freed from her obsession, but only because Sita falls in love with a man and rejects Kate. Perhaps more importantly, the writing style chosen by Millett both reflects and exaggerates the obsessive quality of the relationship; it is a diary style, exploring the actions of others only insofar as they affect the author-protagonist and impinge upon her desires. If the relationship was unhealthy, Millett's writing about it makes the reader feel positively claustrophobic.

Is the resulting story morally or politically educational? Most, if not all, readers of *Sita* are aware of Millett's reputation as a feminist heavyweight. So the main interest of the book (and its selling point, carefully highlighted in the blurbs) lies in the contradiction between the feminist ideals of equality and independence in relationships, and Millett's reality of subservience and utter dependence. The fact that she is subservient toward another woman, not a man, only makes the contradiction sharper. Millett notes that she often felt like a wife or mistress giving up all pride for a few crumbs of love, but curiously enough she does not analyze this contradiction between feminist theory and her practice. Her feminist ideals appear to be totally inoperative, held in abeyance for the duration of the affair. They appear only as guilt feelings or as moral judgements coming from the outside. Millett writes in her diary/book: "Why do I put up with this? Shouldn't I escape and leave with some dignity?" but she pursues her inexorable course from page one to the bitter end, without arriving at any conclusive insight.

Confessions involve recounting one's sins in all the gory details, and then abasing oneself before the confessor (reader) and hoping that by a combination of sincerity and self-abasement one will provoke a pardon. I wonder if Millett, unable to forgive herself for her obsession, felt she had to publicize her humiliation in a lengthy confession and so "earn" the forgiveness of the reading public, in particular feminist readers.

It appears to me that the reader's response is triple. First, we have all been through foolish love at one point or another, and can thus completely identify with Kate the protagonist, suffering with her and being happy when things look up. We reenact what Millett herself calls her "masochism," and our act of reading becomes an obsession paralleling Millett's own. Secondly, as feminists holding certain ideals about equality and autonomy, we stand in judgement over unfeminist love and self-abasement. But, thirdly, we also know how to forgive our sisters, "validating their experience" (as the phrase goes) and patting them on the head saying, "there there, don't be so hard on yourself, we all get into these messes sometimes."

We are a perfect audience. We can be riveted to her tale by identifying with her obsession (which all readers can do), but as feminists we can also both judge and then forgive our fallen sister after hearing her public confession. We go through all sorts of feelings—sympathetic pain, embarrassment, fascination, and forgiveness—but nowhere do we become more critical about the nature of obsessions, nor do we face any challenge to our political and sexual beliefs. As readers, we are not forced to examine either our own experiences of tragic love nor our feminist ideals about non-tragic, companionate love. We simply read obsessively about an obsession that is both ours and not ours, that is Everywoman's lot but that is presented as intensely private; and we go back with a sigh to our obsessed lives.

Finally, in what sense are stories like *Sita* revelations of the sexual truth about women? As Michel Foucault has pointed out, it is only since the late eighteenth century that Western civilization has considered sexual activities as originating in an essential "identity" that is a prime subject for investigation as well as conversation.[12] This notion of an inner core of sexuality is highly problematic. However, even if we granted the existence and importance of an essential sexual core in individuals, how would we know that this is what is revealed by talking? "Talking sex" is a problematic activity, and not just because of modesty and repression. "Talking sex" is a myth; or more accurately, an act of creating a fiction. Speaking/writing about one's own sexuality tends to conform to the rules of either the confessional or the exhibitionist mode (as in pornography), and these two experiential modes are as problematic as the scientific/theoretical mode.

When we say we are talking in a personal way about sex, what we are generally doing is one of the following: humiliating ourselves in the hopes of being granted absolution; bragging about our daring in sexual experimentation; proving our correctness by fitting our acts and thoughts into a particular moral/ethical framework; or apologizing for breaking either traditional moral values or what we perceive to be feminist standards. There is no such thing as straightforward talk about sex that generates shiny "truths" based on one's "experience." Everything that we do and that happens to us is interpreted according to the languages and codes available to us. What we call "experience" is the end result of a complex process of interpretation. It is important to become aware of the rules of these languages, for while we are often skeptical about, for instance, using Freudian theory and Freudian terms to describe our sexuality, we are not as cautious about choosing to use such shopworn linguistic codes as confessional literature or exhibitionist adventure stories.

The problems that I have outlined apply to this book as much as to any other text. I have sometimes felt the fascination of personal revelation on the one hand, and the pull of theoretical knowledge on the other, and have watched myself drastically change writing styles when switching from one mode to another. Despite my efforts at integration, there is still a tension between the two poles of theory and experience, or abstract argument and confessional revelation. This is partly because of my limitations as a writer and partly because no one individual can transcend the mutually exclusive categories of our culture. I only hope that the limitations and tensions which mar this text will spur others to attempt to write integrating the two languages, the two ways in which we approach our sexual existence: theory and experience, subjectivity and objectivity, masculine abstract knowledge and feminine intuition of particulars.

◆

One of the aims in my choice of topics and issues included in this book was to refocus the "sex debates" in order to make a more rigorous discussion possible. For instance, feminists have often addressed ethical and moral sexual questions in the process of debating what pornography is and whether it should be censored. In this book, I analyze pornography as a cultural product in one chapter, while addressing the ethical aspect of sexuality in a separate chapter. I believe that some clarity is gained by separating the two discussions. Another example: some feminist theorists have analyzed the shaping of female desire in and by the mass media. But these cultural analyses have not generally been integrated into the discussion of women's sexual experiences. On the other hand, discussions of sexual experiences often proceed as though we were completely free individuals in complete control of our sexual "choices." In chapter six I shed new light on both the cultural and experiential aspects of our sexuality by integrating the two discussions. I argue there that our desire is indeed socially constructed, but that this does not make us into automatons. We have some latitude in choosing which corner of our culture to inhabit, and in interpreting what we see and read according to our own needs and our political and moral values. We also have some responsibility to connect ethics and pleasure. This is the concern of the last chapter which argues that community-based ethics (as opposed to individual morality) can be integrated into our quest for sexual pleasure.

◆

A word now about the geographical and biographical contexts of this book. First it must be noted that a Canadian critical discourse on sexuality appears to be emerging among feminists, writers, artists, gay activists, and others. Canada is primarily influenced by the United States in all cultural fields, and sexual politics is no exception. But at the same time we retain a healthy sense of difference. We are also influenced by British developments and by French currents of thought (although the French influence in English Canada is surprisingly small given its importance in Quebec). It might well be that we are in a good position to synthesize and go forward, and to learn from all without being dogmatic followers of any one approach. Also, our historical position as an economic and cultural colony—even though it creates such problems as a publishing industry based on the import of American and British books—has given us a very appropriate modesty. While retaining this modesty, however, it might be good for those of us who live in Canada not to assume that all originality comes from New York or Paris, and for those who live elsewhere not to assume that anything that comes from Canada must be derivative and dull.

Secondly, a note on the personal context. There is no pretence that this book is theoretically disinterested or somehow "objective." I write from both a political commitment to the goals of the women's movement and from a specific sexual experience (or, more accurately, from a specific interpretation of what I call "my experience"). However, I have tried to make my experiences and ideas the beginning and not the end of the discussion, and to understand from the inside (as much as it is possible) practical sexual dilemmas that are not affecting me personally at the moment. I have tried as well to give the reader a sense of the basis of theories that I have come to reject. I am also personally familiar with widely different cultural norms—since I am the daughter of Spanish Catholic socialist intellectuals, and now live in an urban progressive enclave in Protestant Ontario—and with various sexual "lifestyles" ranging from heterosexuality to lesbianism, and from marriage to casual flings. (So much for "credentials"!) But what is most important is that although I have been a lesbian feminist for a number of years I have tried to avoid dogmatisms and to leave the door open not just to "the experience of others" but also to feelings and ideas of my own that do not fit with my present self-definition.

◆

The relationship between writer and reader is never as straightforward as schoolteachers would have it. Each text is a site for the author to project an ideal sympathetic reader in her onw image; while each reader looks to the author for maternal advice, reliable knowledge, or simply for exciting stories through which to experience and release her desires. Texts are always constituting particular readers for themselves (and for authors) and simultaneously absorbing the projections and wishes of the readers.

This is especially true in a book about sexuality. Here the writer seeks to disguise her own theoretical contradictions and her ambivalence about personal revelation by imagining a perfectly docile reader who is easily lured by the text. She thinks that because she chose to be vulnerable and take risks, the readers owe her some loyalty. (Even while I knew this was untrue and unfair, believing it helped me get the writing done.) For her part, the reader will undoubtedly seek more than disinterested information. She too has her own experiences, feelings, and frustrated fantasies which she will tend to project onto the text. Some readers may try to find a portrait of her own situation in the text, and finding some portraits that are similar, she may feel that they are not really portraits of herself, and thus not really true.

Some misunderstanding is therefore inevitable. However both of us can at least be aware of the pitfalls and the unhealthy patterns that can make an author-reader relationship sour and stagnant, instead of dynamic and fruitful. As a writer, I have tried to avoid the two methods most commonly used in texts about sexuality: blanket generalizations stated in an academic voice, on the one hand, and juicy stories told in a seductive voice, on the other. Authorial authoritarianism is an ever-present danger. As a feminist I have been aggravated by its existence in male texts for a long time. However, the apparently innocuous ploy of revealing raw sexual experience is equally questionable. It lures and seduces instead of convincing, and succeeds if it gets the reader to identify with the story without actually thinking it through. Hence, in both my "theoretical" and my "experiential" writings I attempt to go beyond mere authority and mere seduction. Yet it is impossible to completely avoid these traditional modes of addressing the reader, especially since she is accustomed to being addressed precisely in these two ways.

The reader, then—this means you—has the task of detecting both authority and seduction wherever they threaten to exercise their power. The reader also has to avoid the opposite trap, which consists in unmasking the printed word as seducer and rejecting its advances before giving the argument a fair hearing. This kind of reaction is usually expressed in words like, "You may work like that, but not me, period." A premature denial of agreement, of commonality, can be due to a prejudice about the experience or view just encountered, or to a simple fear of the unknown. Fear and prejudice in the sexual sphere cannot be banished from the reader's mind at will, but one can learn to distinguish those reactions in oneself and see them for what they are.

In conclusion, I do not want disciples to absorb my theories on authority; I do not want weak-willed souls who will submerge their own desires in the erotic appeal of the text; and I do not want prudish minds who will reject out of hand anything that does not fit with what they think they have experienced. Which is not to say that I want to abolish the necessarily erotic connection between reader and writer; far from it. I just want it to be an egalitarian and open-ended match, in which there is both struggle and identification. Both partners have to be self-conscious about the fantasies and projections imposed on the text and on each other; both have to be open to the unexpected, to the knowledge we did not know we had, the desire for which we had no name.

But in order to fully explain my vision of the reader/writer relationship as an erotic connection, I have to go on to the discussion of erotic interaction in general, the topic of the first chapter.

◆

BODY AND EROTIC POWER

To THINK AND TALK ABOUT SEXUALITY is first of all to think and talk about bodies. Long before any conscious thoughts of sex cross our minds, we all have a sense of our physical, bodily identity. Even as children we develop a sense of how we feel as a human body and how we appear to others.

As three- or four-year-olds learn both how to use their bodies and how to create an image, one of their first worries is: what is proper for a girl? what is proper for a boy? Boys have to suffer the tyranny of the macho model, and this is especially hard for those who are happier doing "sissy" things. But at least their training is meant to give them power. Girls' training is by contrast designed to render them powerless, both in the real world and in their own imaginations.

A three-year-old girl might be boisterous, uninhibited, and perhaps rough or "bossy" when she plays with other children. As she begins to attend school and spend those long Canadian winter evenings in front of the television, she absorbs the messages that are given off like radiation from all these places. Girls shouldn't be bossy. Girls should be nice. Girls should be quiet, not loud. Girls cry; boys don't. Girls take care of little brothers and pets; boys are cruel to small animals and to children who are smaller than they. Girls play house; boys play sports.

What are the implications of this for girls' physical and sexual self-image? Let me try to refer to my own experience. When I was a child, I had a rather indistinct notion of what I was supposed to be as a grown-up woman (perhaps because we didn't have a TV set). But I definitely knew what I *wasn't* supposed to be. I was not supposed to play soccer, even though it was my favourite game. I was not supposed to yell or dirty my clothes. I was not supposed to work up a sweat, except maybe on Sunday afternoons if I was wearing old jeans. I was not supposed to be strong. And I was not supposed to invent games for my younger sister and I to play together. Instead I was expected to fit into my older brother's orderly fantasies, and to play whatever role he assigned me. So I would obediently listen to my brother tell us about every different kind of jet plane in existence, bored to tears and itching to go outdoors. And after a while I might rebel and go out, causing a ruckus in my attempt to take my sister along.

Fortunately, my mother did not believe in the theory of Proper Girlhood. She didn't care that I preferred to play "cowboys and Indians" to playing with dolls. But even though my mother let things be, the whole world around me gave me a very clear message: my fantasies about becoming a sports star could only flourish if I turned myself into a young man in my imagination. When my sister and I constructed an elaborate fantasy world in which we were strong heroes, we went by the ludicrous names of Tom and Harry (especially ludicrous because we grew up in Spain). In Franco's Spain, there were no such things as school psychologists—which was probably a good thing for my sister and I. But if there had been a school psychologist, he would have said that I was experiencing confusion in regard to my gender identity. He would have looked at me through his glasses, stroked his beard, and asked: why did I have contempt for dolls? And why did I hate the colour pink? Indeed, abnormal symptoms were everywhere.

Anyone of sound common sense could have seen I wasn't secretly longing for a male body. I was not rejecting the ovaries and uterus I did not know. I was simply longing to be strong, tough, knowledgeable, and in charge of things. Some of my desires, such as the desire for knowledge, could be more or less fulfilled, for instance by reading. But the desire to be strong was constantly thwarted, and was therefore very prominent in my consciousness.

Being strong allows you to do things yourself. Being strong means that you feel good, and as a result look good. It is thus completely at odds with the theory of Proper Girlhood. That theory states that if you go through the rituals of feminine beauty, then you will *look* good, and as a prize you may feel good, if you are not too busy worrying about the myriad things that might conceivably have gone wrong with your appearance since the last time you looked in the mirror. Looking good is, according to the theory, the main purpose of a girl's life, while feeling good is a secondary effect.

The dichotomy between feeling strong and looking good is related to a more basic dichotomy: doing versus being observed, subject versus object. This does not mean that all concern for one's appearance arises out of a desire to be an inert object. There is a valid pride in one's appearance which is an active affirmation of oneself in the world. But the problem for women is that the concern for one's appearance often takes precedence over other concerns. Moreover, the standards by which we measure our appearance are an externally imposed set of impossible ideals. They are not designed to increase our strength and beauty. Part of the reason for trying to imitate the mythical Perfect Body is that we want to be attractive to men; but the process of creating a proper feminine appearance often goes far beyond what any one man would expect from a particular woman. We also internalize society's standards, and begin to sincerely *feel* wrong when we do not comply with a particular rule about appearance. We are not judged only by men; we ourselves look critically at our own bodies (and those of other women) from the standpoint of Man in general, as articulated by Madison Avenue and Hollywood.

Scene #1

The locker room at the local Y.W.C.A.. After an exercise class, women walk about in various states of undress. The routine is as follows: from the locker to the shower to the whirlpool, then to the shower again, to the hair dryer, on to the scales, and back to the locker to get dressed. A red-haired woman of about thirty, in good physical condition, sighs as she walks by the full-length mirror on her way to the whirlpool. She looks at herself, frowns, and wraps her large towel even tighter around her chest. Ten minutes later, relaxed from the whirlpool, she walks back, this time without any towels to shield her from the other women's glances or from the all-powerful mirror. This time she looks in an absentminded way in the general direction of the mirror, and an almost invisible smile crosses her face. She appears to be admiring her own breasts. But after she returns to the locker and puts on her underwear she decides to weigh herself. The scales reveal that she is two pounds heavier than she was on Tuesday. The frown returns, and stays as she puts on her clothes and combs her hair. All of a sudden she is tired.

Women are at war with their bodies. This is both because they are bodies and subject to such ravages of age as stretch marks and wrinkles, and because they are *women's* bodies. Inside, women's bodies are full of disgusting fluids, slimy and unclean surfaces and nameless substances. They constantly embarrass us by bleeding once a month, bloating before they bleed and causing us aches and pains. But even the outside, the surface which is the place of beauty, fails us. Women's bodies are generally rounded, not straight as rods, and they have curves not only around the breasts but also around the buttocks and thighs. Given current definitions of beauty it is inevitable that 95 percent of the world's women will feel inadequate and downright ugly. It is frightening to think just how deeply many women despise their own bodies, hate them, are at war with them. It is frightening, but necessary to confront this fact if we are going to learn how to feel good.

In our exaggerated, overly critical evaluation of our own bodies, the irrational fear of fat probably plays a larger role than any other factor, even aging. It is not uncommon for a woman who weighs 110 pounds and is approaching skinniness to have a self-image better suited to a beached whale. The woman in question would not be judged as overweight by her boyfriend or by society at large, but her own internalized criteria distort her real image like a convex mirror. She always looks too fat in her own eyes, and she equates fatness with ugliness, laziness, sloth, social isolation, even depression.

Scene #2

A fourteen-year-old girl, in good physical shape, is sitting down on the edge of her bed. She is about to get dressed to go to school, after which she has a basketball game. She puts on her underwear and one knee sock, and as she pulls up the other sock she looks down at her thighs. She stares. Her arms and legs and even her upper body are all right, she thinks, but look at those thighs. Why can't they be firm? Why do they have to give out like that, with all that disgusting flesh that spreads out when you sit down? If only she could get rid of that rounded excess, then everything would be fine. She imagines for a brief moment what it would be like to take a magic razor, that did not hurt or draw blood, and cut out her excess flesh. Then she could reshape her body like a sculptor working on marble. Then it would be perfect.

The girl in question was me. It is not surprising that a few months after the incident described above I developed a very serious case of anorexia, which destroyed my health for two years and made me end up in a hospital in a state of near-starvation. However, in the war against my own body, fatness was not the only or even the most important enemy. Once I became truly skinny I knew perfectly well that I would look much better with more pounds of flesh on my all-too-visible bones. But after I had gotten rid of each and every one of my fat cells, I began to get off on not eating, to enjoy starvation as an end in itself. I came to relish upsetting my family, being stared at, and most importantly having perfect control over my base instincts. I knew my parents wanted me to eat, and so I associated the instinct to eat with *their* desires, not mine. Instead, "I" was the mystical, starving self, in battle against the base instincts. I would refrain not just from eating but even from drinking water. Calories were only the enemy's foot soldiers; the real enemy I was fighting against was my body, my instincts, my desires. And I almost won.

Once I was thirty pounds underweight, my desperate parents took me to the Hospital for Sick Children in Toronto. I was a precocious, well-read fifteen-year-old, and being imprisoned in a ward full of eight-year-old diabetics and Cystic Fibrosis cases was not my idea of a mystical experience. The staff never spoke to me about my illness, or even named it, but made it clear that I could only get out of the hospital if I gained ten pounds. I knew they didn't particularly care if I lived or died, so it didn't seem to be worth it to prove any points by not eating. And so I ate and ate, wolfing down even the starchy chocolate puddings they served for dessert. After a couple of weeks I was released, ten pounds heavier but not an ounce wiser.

Not everyone goes to such extremes, of course. But going to and through that extreme forced me to look at the weird dynamic of self-mastery that I had developed. It took me many years (and I certainly resisted it) but eventually I did begin to create more positive concepts of the body, of eating, of attractiveness, and of the relation between mind and instinct. In this sense it is not coincidental that I only began to truly overcome my anorexia when I began to have sexual relationships. As I developed a positive sense of my own sexuality, the anorexic distinction between the true "I" and the base instincts collapsed.

For many girls the instinct that has to be controlled is not so much lust but hunger. Boys are encouraged to control themselves, to refrain from raping their girlfriends or leering at women in the streets. But girls are not supposed to have an active sexuality anyway. By an interesting sleight-of-hand, the battle for self-control takes place in the kitchen rather than under the sheets. Donuts and ice cream are the adolescent girl's mortal sins. We are taught that "pigging out" is bad, but we are not taught the pleasures of good eating and as a result we have no natural thermometer to tell us what we want to eat or when. Deprived of the joy of good cooking and eating, all we know about food is that most of it is fattening. We grow up locked into a battle between sugar and starch on the one hand, and feminine beauty on the other. Both poles of this opposition are equally artificial, but the effect is to make it seem that beauty and success are only achieved by stamping out the most basic natural instinct: hunger. And so many girls spend their teenage years crushing their hunger and confusing their system by occasional feasts of sugar. No wonder we have trouble being "natural" about sex.

THE DIALECTIC
OF EROTIC RECOGNITION

The peculiar tendency of young women to displace their anxieties about the body and its desires away from sex and toward food may to some extent be explained by the larger problem of the role that sex plays in our society. This problem is the apparent paradox whereby our society is simultaneously highly sexualized and highly repressed. Let us first deal with the sexualization.

We all grow up surrounded by sexual and sexy images, and by a constant blare of propaganda that promotes sexual bliss as the ultimate human pursuit. From soft-core porn to *Women's Day* articles about the importance of good sex in marriage, most mass-produced cultural products have a clear message about sex: it is extremely important. It may be seen as wholly good (*Playboy*), as bad (traditional religion) or as a mixed bag of good and bad (Ann Landers), but all agree on its supreme importance.

People did not always see sex in this light. Only in the late nineteenth and especially in the twentieth century has sex come to play this crucial role. Our century has developed a special science of sex, and the other human sciences have increasingly come to regard all human activity as the outward expression of hidden sexual truths.[1] Furthermore, the incredible growth in the consumer market has necessitated exploiting sexual desires and fantasies as much as possible in order to stimulate consumer demand.

Other social factors are involved in this sexualization of society, such as the simultaneous decline both in traditional religion and in the traditional romantic view of sex as justified only by love. But whatever the causes—and it would take a whole book to begin to outline them—the fact remains that sex is an important lubricant for the smooth functioning of consumer capitalism, both in being itself packaged and marketed, and in its function as an attractive additive to other products.

However, we would be making a serious error if we thought that because sex appears to be everywhere, repression and sexual ignorance are no longer problems. A sexualized society does not guarantee sexual pleasure for individuals. Sex is not any one thing or homogeneous substance whose presence can be measured in any one place and time. Rather, "sex" refers both to a whole series of human possibilities and practices, and to their cultural expression. In our own society certain types of sex are prevalent in and very much encouraged by mainstream culture, while other sexual possibilities are virtually invisible. In practicing the latter one becomes a member of a stigmatized minority. And, as we shall discuss shortly, what one means by the very word "sex" is different according to one's gender, sexual orientation, and to some extent class and race. Thus, it makes little sense to argue about whether there is too much repression or too much permissiveness in general. What we can ask is: how have the prevalent views about the meaning and importance of sex changed over the years? And what have been the consequences of what one writer has called "the modernization of sex"[2] for society at large and for women as an oppressed group?

As many feminists have already noted, the modernization of sex has had contradictory effects on women's lives and on our self-image. On the one hand, the twentieth century has "discovered" women's sexual pleasure. The significance of the studies by Masters and Johnson, Shere Hite and others ought not to be underestimated by cynical or expert-weary feminists. There is no doubt that many millions of women now expect sexual pleasure in their lives, and many are willing to struggle to obtain it. The expectation of sexual happiness, both in marriage and in non-marriage relationships, is widely accepted. Large numbers of men have begun to alter age-old sexual practices in order to fulfil these new expectations of female pleasure. They may do so grudgingly, half-heartedly, or without ever directly asking women what they want. But there is an expectation that sex is supposed to produce pleasure for women as well as men, and this is a very significant historical change.

But on the other hand, the (hetero)sexualization of social relations, and the emphasis on the sexual aspect of all relations, has in some ways helped to create yet another ideological prison for women. Women are now expected to be sexual athletes, to "work at" sex, and to live up to unrealistic expectations of multiple orgasms. While many women may be experiencing more physical pleasure than their mothers did, they are also subject to new pressures, and often feel the ideal of the sexually liberated woman as an externally imposed standard. When sex becomes all-important, even if there is an emphasis on mutuality in heterosexual relationships women are still "the sex." Changes in sexual behaviour and ideology thus have more of an impact on women than on men, simply because sex (and relationships) continue to be regarded as women's speciality.

Because women are more defined by sexuality than men, sexuality is for us a more dangerous territory. Even when pregnancy is not a factor, women as a group are still risking more than men when we make changes in our sexual lives. This is partly because public opinion still stigmatizes "loose" or "frigid" women, and so we have to be careful if we do not want to lose the approval of others. Even more important, however, are our emotional difficulties around sex and relationships. We tend to gain more self-definition from relationships than men do; and at the purely sexual level, we often take a long time to be truly comfortable in/with our bodies and desires. Despite all the propaganda about sex being simple and matter-of-fact, we know it is not; there are many (and conflicting) social forces that continue to problematize sex and hinder the development of an "innocent" sexuality.

The problems brought about by the historical process of the modernization of sex are compounded by psychological factors that make sexuality problematic for everyone but especially for women.

THE DIALECTIC OF DESIRE [3]

The human sexual urge is not only a physiological fact. Through our sexual feelings and relations we play out basic psychological dynamics, and especially in our era, with the importance given to sexuality for self-realization. The "modernization of sex" that we described in the previous section is not only an ideology influencing us from the outside; we *feel* sex to be crucial to our psychological growth, and to that extent it really is crucial. Our society simply does not provide alternative ways for certain physiological needs to be met outside sexual relationships. The person who is celibate by choice or by necessity has to spend a great deal of time and energy trying to find alternatives. In physiological terms, we could do just fine without sex (and masturbation has been proven to be physiologically more effective, at least for women) but the emotional component is difficult to replace.

One of the most important emotional processes that gets played out in sex is the desire to both know someone truly and to be fully known by her/him. This desire for acknowledgment and for knowledge, for "the truth," has been linked to eroticism by philosophers from Plato to Freud. But what Freud pointed out is that this is not only, or even primarily, an intellectual process. When we seek to be acknowledged and known by another it is not only for the sake of truth: it is also for the sake of power. An individual has no power unless there is an Other to recognize one's individuality and one's actions. As the philosopher Hegel put it, we only really become subjects when our actions are seen and known by other subjects who can then confirm in an objective way our claim to be subjects.

In sexual or non-sexual relations, we all need to be autonomous human beings and to be acknowledged as independent and powerful. In an erotic situation this would mean we all want to be the lover, the one in control, the subject who initiates sex. But we also have an equally strong need to give up our human power, to surrender it to a stronger being who will "take" us and relieve us of the tremendous responsibility of being active, of making choices. The need to assert our sexual power and overwhelm someone is perpetually shifting, giving way to the deep longing to be engulfed, to return to the womb, to be both overpowered and protected.

This dialectic, this interplay of opposites, echoes the infant's struggle to become independent of the mother while at the same time wanting to have her love and protection. In the case of boys, who are told explicitly and implicitly that they are to become men, i.e. radically unlike the mother, there is a tendency for the tension between independence and fusion to be resolved into a permanent (and undialectical) wish to dominate others, especially women. The boy dislikes being dependent on the mother, and elaborates a counter-fantasy in which he is all-powerful and can exert his will over all women. Girls also go through this differentiation process, but they cannot see the mother as radically other. They thus tend to identify more with her, and so with other sources of nurture and authority, even as they try to become more powerful and independent. As Nancy Chodorow has pointed out, many of these psychological differences between girls and boys would be far less marked if women were not the sole nurturers of young children.[4]

The mother/child relationship and all its unresolved contradictions inevitably shape the power dynamics of erotic relationships. Because boys are almost universally brought up by women, and because they are taught to see their gender as essential to their self-definition, they grow up tending to see the objects of their desire as fundamentally Other. The boy tends to collapse his inevitable dependence on adults with dependence on women, especially strong, maternal women. He then resents this dependence and grows hostile to women in general. Women, on the other hand, will not be quite as intent on objectifying the Other, or on rejecting parental figures. This could be a very positive characteristic if it were counterbalanced by a strong sense of self. Unfortunately, however, socialization intervenes to prevent women from developing this. The woman who has been traditionally brought up and successfully socialized will therefore identify with the Other's desire and pleasure *instead of* developing her own desires. Her much-vaunted selflessness, which could be very positive, is turned into a negative characteristic when women live simply for and through their men. In fact one could argue that selflessness turns into its opposite, for if the woman no longer has any desires other than those of her husband/son, her working to achieve these is nothing but her peculiar way to fulfilment. We can all probably think of some examples of women who have fallen into this trap by virtue of being perfect wives or perfect mothers.

It is sexist social relations that push women into expressing only the "submissive" side of the dialectic of eroticism. It is a sexist social structure which divides the two poles from one another, and assigns to men the permanent role of hunter/lover/subject, while confining women to that of hunted/beloved/object. In our rigidly gendered society, erotic interactions tend to stagnate: the lover cannot become the beloved, the protector cannot seek protection. Men are cast automatically into the "strong" role, and women are, without any struggle, put into the role of the one who is taken, the one who surrenders. In specific circumstances the roles may be reversed, but this always involves struggling against what is "normal," going against the grain. In movies depicting men who are under the thumb of women they love, this situation is seen as something in need of explanation, whereas the opposite situation is presented as "natural."

In "normal" circumstances men are sexy because they have male social power. The images of male eroticism directed at women are diverse because the forms of male power are diverse: the violent, dark hero of a Harlequin romance is erotic because of his raw physical and psychological power, while the Young Doctors in Love are erotic in a nice, safe, suburban kind of way. Michael Jackson, Aristotle Onassis, and Prince Charles are all constructed as desirable (or, as women's magazines tactfully put it, "eligible"). Their sex appeal is different depending on the social meaning of their respective roles, but the one common denominator is that power contributes to a man's sex appeal.

Women, on the other hand, are not supposed to exercise any active power. We are not supposed to initiate sexual play, and indeed are not even granted the unconditional right to put an end to the erotic initiative of the male. But we do have a very indirect and limited form of power: the power of surrender. Now, to make surrender into a form of power, we have to make it count. We have to hold out, play hard to get, extend the courtship and postpone sex. In this way we exercise an indirect and mostly passive form of power over the aggressor, a kind of power best symbolized by the sexist expression "feminine wiles."

Surrender is our peculiarly feminine form of power. It is therefore also our peculiarly feminine eroticism. The guardedness of the hunted has to be covered in a sexual gloss, as does the strength of the hunter. However, this is a far cry from saying that feminine women are weakly passive. It takes a lot of intelligence, skill and energy to play the feminine role, and to get the most out of the withholding or granting of one's consent. A woman who is completely passive, and does not discriminate among suitors, has only a low-quality form of sexual appeal. The sexiest women in traditional culture are those who maximize their passive power play with their own sex appeal as one would play the stock market, careful about timing and never in a rush to sell right away. Similarly, a woman who is completely naked is not as sexy as one who is almost naked, and who manipulates the suitor by promising or enticing to reveal all at the right time and place. Many of the women who claim not to need feminism are precisely those who have learned so well to maximize their passive power that it almost looks and feels like active power.

I began this section by stating that one of the most important aspects of eroticism was the urge to know and be known, i.e. the desire for recognition. Now, we as human beings can only be recognized by other human beings, preferably social equals. An object, an inert thing, cannot give us any recognition. Thus if a man succeeds in turning a woman into a quasi-object, if he robs her of social power and makes her completely dependent on him, his own desire for recognition will be frustrated. For she has been made virtually non-human and her recognition is worth nothing. His desire for domination, for turning others into mere instruments for his every whim, may be fulfilled but his equally strong desire for recognition is necessarily frustrated. As Jessica Benjamin points out, one possible reason for male sexual violence against women is precisely the rage experienced by men who, having succeeded in dominating women and subjecting them to their will, no longer gain any pleasure from that submission. When a woman no longer has a will of her own, tangling with her and forcing her into submission is no longer a challenge. This particular dialectic of domination does not resolve itself into a mutual recognition of equals, as might be the case when the individuals involved are social equals. Then their erotic play, involving submission and conquest, takes place in the context of acknowledging each other's individuality and humanness. In a situation of macho husband and submissive wife, the erotic struggle is no longer a dialectical interplay and has indeed lost its playful character. It is rather a one-way descent into extreme roles, which are then the conditions for the possibility of extreme violence on the one hand and extreme masochism on the other.[5]

Thus, we see the contradiction inherent in the erotic of male power. On the one hand, a man's potential use of violence is part of his sexiness. But on the other hand, the *actual* use of brute force is not erotic, for women especially but even for men themselves. Brute force is the substitute for mutual recognition, the substitute that is used when the two partners are not fully equal and fully human. Force destroys the possibility of mutual recognition. The violated woman becomes an object, and cannot give the acknowledgment craved by the male aggressor. If the male master continues to assert his power through violence, the female slave will become a corpse, lifeless and therefore utterly unable to acknowledge his mastery. The male's victory is therefore also his defeat.[6] (This dynamic, incidentally, is probably the main reason why pornography almost always makes a show of having the woman actively consent to violent acts against her—it is not so much out of deference to women, but because the male's desire for power would ultimately be frustrated if she were reduced to an inert object.)

For erotic recognition to be possible, both people involved have to be fully human. They also have to be prepared to recognize the other as such. This does not mean they have to be mathematically equal, and that we can only have relationships with people of the same gender, age, race, and social class. In many cases differences add to erotic appeal (although, paradoxically, similarities do as well). The point is that these differences must not be seen as rigid and permanent indications of one's "natural" role; rather, they must be seen as elements in an erotic play whose aim is to subvert the usual social meanings of those differences. A small example: even if a heterosexual woman is quite happy having intercourse while on her back, she might well want to reverse the "normal" position and be on top for a while, just to see what it feels like to be the one who controls the rhythm during intercourse. Once she is comfortable in the "on top" position, she might not use it very often, but at least she will know that there is no intrinsic reason why men should be on top. And her male partner might have learned something too.

The emphasis, then, must be on dynamic change. We must experiment with the rituals and symbols of eroticism so that the dynamic of sexual power can lead to a true mutual recognition of people who are fully human and therefore equal, without having to be the same.

Many feminists have pointed out that the eroticization of male power, for example in pornography, helps to prop up patriarchy by making it sexy. And so many feminists have come to the conclusion that we have to purify sexuality and eliminate all power from erotic play. I think this is misguided. In my view it is not power itself which is inherently bad, but rather the way in which power gets used by one gender against another, and by one individual against another. In our society, economic as well as erotic power are used to exploit people who have less power. But we cannot abolish economic power itself. What we can do is change economic relations so that economic power rests in the collectivity and cannot be used by one person or group against another. Similarly, erotic power has come to mean rape and violence against women. But are we being realistic when we envisage a feminist society in which there is no erotic power, no lust, and where everything is enveloped in the soft mists of tenderness and mutual nurturing?

Where there is strong eroticism, there is power. The point is that we have to change gender relations (and race and class relations as well) so that one person's power is not another's humiliation. We have to make sure that everyone can be both the lover and the beloved, the protector and the protected, the one who takes and the one who surrenders. This will involve social change, not just an improvement in attitudes. At present it is difficult for a heterosexual woman to "freely" give in to her desire to be sexually overwhelmed, because part of the backdrop is a society in which a woman is raped every few minutes. We have to collectivize and equalize power. Then we will be free to really play, to really explore the possibilities of the dialectic of desire.

It is not a question of abolishing sexual power but rather subverting and transforming it. In this way we will be more in control of the dialectic, more free to make choices and changes and to experiment without undue fear. Erotic power has to be detached from the bedrock of patriarchal social relations; it has to be used to eroticize equality—which is by no means synonymous with sameness—rather than inequality.

The feminist vision of eroticism is not some sort of egalitarian, homogenized boredom in which nobody overwhelms others and in which self-surrender is prohibited. The feminist vision (or perhaps I should say, my feminist vision) tries to integrate the two poles—autonomy and responsibility, power and surrender. And this for men as well as women.

But this does not mean that we have to be mechanistic about our roles: active 50 percent of the time, passive 50 percent of the time. A less mechanistic approach would involve not only "taking turns" but being sensitive to the fact that when one is being sexually "passive," that does not mean one is powerless and weak, and one is being "active" one is not necessarily being domineering or abusive.

A dynamic sense of equality would involve each of the partners identifying with the other's pleasure, watching and feeling how the "passive" or "active" pleasure of one's lover develops fully, ripens, and unexpectedly turns into its opposite. Dynamic equality certainly begins with an acknowledgment that both partners have a right to pleasure, and that since simultaneous orgasms are not the norm, there may have to be a certain amount of turn-taking. But once that has been established it would be counter-productive to start keeping track of who makes love to whom with a stopwatch. Dynamic equality is about sharing sexual power, not about making sure everyone has exactly the same number of orgasms as the other person. Part of that sharing is the identification with the other's pleasure, such that we can sometimes feel satisfied with and by the other's orgasm.

This identification is not an abolition of all difference. There is always a certain tension between giving and receiving, being on top and being on the bottom, and these differences will always be an integral part of eroticism. But the identification allows for a mutual recognition of two human subjects who recognize one another as being autonomous, and who see all the erotic possibilities developed in lovemaking as belonging in some way to both partners. In other words, the various possibilities of human erotic play are developed in a situation in which each role or possibility (including what we think of as "male" and "female") is actualized by differentiation against its opposite, its complementary pleasure. Once developed, however, the possibilities belong to both partners, and can be experienced by each as his/her own. Women have been brought up to identify primarily with such passive pleasures as being penetrated, but there is no reason why we cannot learn to use our imagination and feel the pleasure of "taking" someone. To some extent this involves being physically adventurous, but it can also mean thinking and feeling things differently. As some feminists have pointed out, intercourse in the missionary position does not have to mean "passive woman being fucked by aggressive male." It could just as easily be experienced as "strong woman engulfing a hesitant male."

There is no reason then for feminists to make a fetish out of quantitative equality or sameness in sexuality, just because traditional thinking emphasizes inequality and domination. Similarly, we must not react against our long experience of being treated as sexual objects by going to the other extreme and denying any and all forms of objectification, thus putting ourselves in the impossible position of pure subjects. Let me explain.

As feminists, we have tried to increase women's assertiveness and men's emotional expressiveness in an attempt to reduce gender inequality as much as possible. And we have insisted that women are not the objects of man's desire, but human subjects in our own right. However, a minimum of "objectification" is necessary for erotic interaction, and indeed for any interaction. When we choose what clothes to wear for the day or how to cut our hair, when we try to get a tan or disdain the attempt, we are objectifying ourselves, that is, presenting ourselves as a particular object in the world. We all want to control our appearance, the way in which we present ourselves as objects for others to see. Similarly, when we find someone attractive we are not drawn solely to that person's innermost soul, but also to a particular body. So we objectify ourselves and others all the time.

As feminists, what we properly object to is the kind of objectification found in pornography whereby women are turned into *mere* objects, anonymous creatures with no will of their own, no names and no distinctive features. When women are presented *only* as objects then we are clearly being dehumanized. But our revulsion at this kind of "bad"objectification should not make us fall into the untenable extreme of rejecting all objectification. We are not disembodied souls, and would probably not enjoy ourselves if we were.

The task is not to reject all objectification in favour of an impossible ideal of pure subjectivity, but rather to integrate the two aspects of human existence. The task is to remain a full human subject even while someone is considering us as a potential erotic object, and vice versa. An eroticism that is both sexy and egalitarian is one in which both partners are simultaneously subject and object, for one another as well as for themselves.

This approach assumes that both partners recognize one another as social equals, or in any case equivalents. This sounds easy enough, but it is not easy to get rid of the stereotypes we have inherited—and not just of sex and gender. A highly educated lover might very easily make certain assumptions about the mental and emotional range of a less educated lover; people of different races will inherit all the tensions that have marked social relations between their respective races, and they will not be able to transcend those tensions by simply saying "but we deal with each other as individuals." It is impossible to ignore differences that carry a great deal of social meaning, and even if it were, our task as people who care about equality is to undermine social inequality, not just ignore it, in our emotional life.

There are many women today, from all walks of life and not necessarily all card-carrying feminists, who are doing precisely that in their sexual lives: trying to undermine the inherited inequalities that shape our erotic life. There are also some men who are involved in this project, usually in conjunction with women lovers. Let us then continue our discussion of erotic equality without sameness, of erotic difference without domination, in the specific context of the theory and practice of heterosexuality.

◆

CHAPTER TWO

HETEROSEXUALITY: CONTESTED GROUND

I T IS NOT EASY to write generally about heterosexuality. Relations between men and women have been subject to much scrutiny over the past twenty years and although traditional ideas and practices continue to hold sway in some quarters there are other circles in which little can be taken for granted any more. These different perspectives do not merely coexist in peaceful détente. Even if there are some "islands" of both traditionalism and feminism where people live without many direct, personal challenges to their beliefs, by and large we are all living in an ideological battlefield. The combined effect of skyrocketing divorce rates and feminist ideas has produced a counter-attack by the traditionalists, who have become increasingly shrill about the divine rights of husbands. This rightwing backlash is a desperate reaction to a situation in which the breadwinner husband/dependent wife model has become economically unfeasible for the vast majority of couples as well as emotionally unsatisfying for many women.

We live therefore in a very polarized situation, with different groups contending for the power to define heterosexuality and the family. Within each camp people strategize about how to strengthen their forces and how to improve their position on the field; they react to one another's ideology and on occasion are influenced by ideas from the "enemy" camp. All this means that, reassurances of sex and family experts notwithstanding, we cannot speak confidently about heterosexuality in general. Both the ideas about it and the corresponding sexual and social practices are quite diverse and we are in a process of struggle and change.

Furthermore, we see many gaps between theory and practice. Some women have embraced the idea of an egalitarian heterosexuality that stresses choice and creativity, but in their own lives fall into traditional gender roles which they experience as "natural." On the other hand, many women who have sincerely believed in traditional concepts of marriage are finding themselves by design or by accident in unorthodox situations that are not part of the plan. Faced with such realities as an unwanted pregnancy, a daughter who comes out as a lesbian, or a divorce, women who have led "traditional" lives sometimes show a remarkable degree of flexibility and inventiveness. So we cannot assume that all women with feminist beliefs have what one might describe as feminist relationships, or that women who are married and go to church on Sundays necessarily restrict themselves to monogamous heterosexuality in the missionary position.

It might be useful first to pause and consider one of the most prevalent myths used by the anti-feminists in the ideological struggle to define heterosexuality. It is a myth that often lingers in the hearts if not the minds of feminists, and so must be explicitly refuted if we are to make a fresh start. This myth comes in many guises but the common denominator is an appeal to Nature to legitimize a certain traditional definition of heterosexuality as "natural" and therefore inevitable, good, and not to be argued about or criticized. Arguments for Nature try to remove heterosexuality from the realm of politics and history and put it safely away on a high shelf marked "Mother Nature: things that just are."

An influential exponent of this argument for Nature is "America's number one counsellor," Dr. Joyce Brothers. In her 1981 book entitled *What Every Woman Should Know About Men* she blithely "deduces" the traditional nuclear family from her perception of "primitive" human life. Appealing to our stereotype of "cavemen," she writes:

> It is as if way back in prehistory Mother Nature had searched for the most effective way of protecting mothers and children. Without someone to provide food for and defend the mother and child, they were at the mercy of wild beasts and predatory males. . . . The obvious source of protection and provisions was the male. But how to keep him around?
>
> Mother Nature's solution was sex. Sex on tap, so to speak.

The day-in, day-out sexual availability of the human female created what scientists call a pair bond and most of us call love. The nuclear family was born.[1]

Let us unpack the assumptions and values contained in this unfortunately typical piece of popular "scientific" writing.

• "Mother" Nature is portrayed as a manipulative mother-in-law. This is anthropomorphism at its worst, where Nature is not only a human female but an "old hag" who manipulates people for her own purposes.

• Men are portrayed as naturally predatory and obsessed with sex. Dr. Brothers is apparently relying here on some now-discredited anthropological studies that claimed to show it was the aggressiveness and sexual jealousy of the male that pushed us along the evolutionary path and made us into a civilized species. The myth of "Man the Hunter" has been successfully challenged by feminist anthropologists and primatologists. Male anthropologists have tended to assume that for example a social system could be understood by looking at the *men* in the system, and that competition and aggression were "natural" and beneficial to the species. Without going into details about how this traditional view was challenged, suffice it to say that now only the die-hards in the anthropological profession would see even a grain of truth in Dr. Brothers's description.[2]

• Further, even if her description were accurate there is a logical error in her argument. If males were so predatory, why would women turn to them as the "obvious source" of protection? A pack of dogs would be much more appropriate.

• The women in Dr. Brothers's prehistory appear to have not sexual feelings but only sexual "availability." Now, given that many female primates show clear signs of sexual pleasure, and some species even exhibit what can be interpreted as female orgasms, one wonders why women in prehistory would have such a passive sexuality. But the myth is that women do not really want sex, and exchange sexual favours only for male protection, while men do not really want to nurture but will reluctantly provide protection for the sake of sex. There is a lapse here in the logic of how the nuclear family can emerge from this coming together of two such vastly different beings with such completely different purposes in mind.

• Finally, it seems clear that according to Dr. Brothers the only "natural" expression of human sexuality is monogamous heterosexuality within a nuclear family. By trying to ground her view of heterosexuality in "Mother Nature" she confines all other possibilities to the obscurity of non-natural or anti-natural human behaviour. In the rest of her book she downplays the family and does not insist on children in the way the Pope does. But she certainly believes that real sex is heterosexual sex, and real love is heterosexual love.

This belief in the naturalness of heterosexuality is so commonly accepted that we do not even notice it. (See chapter three for more on the problem of invisibility.) These days it is seldom articulated in its most blatant forms. But in its more sophisticated and subtle versions, which de-emphasize reproduction and stress sex itself, it continues to exercise a great deal of influence not just over our thoughts but over our very feelings. We feel it is somehow right for men and women to be attracted to one another precisely because they are men or women. We smile on young happy heterosexual couples and we attend wedding celebrations, regardless of the actual interactions between the two people in question. By contrast, we feel uncomfortable when rules about monogamy and exclusive heterosexuality are broken, and feel compelled to find explanations for why woman A has so many lovers or why man B is attracted to men. But if A and B join up as a stable, monogamous couple, then we cease to ask questions. Their relationship, like Dr. Brothers's primitive society, simply is.

One of the most crucial building blocks of the traditional view of natural heterosexuality is the idea that penises and vaginas "go together" or "are meant for each other," and that erotic attraction between men and women is only the psychological manifestation of the physiological urge to engage in intercourse. There are several problems with this view. First, it portrays men and women as the dupes of their own physiology and considers eroticism as a mere cover-up for Nature's reproductive aims. People are thus dehumanized, first by being reduced to one sexual organ and then by having those sexual organs reduced to the status of reproductive tools. Secondly, it ignores the specificity of sex by collapsing it into reproduction. This implicitly devalues not only homosexuality but all non-reproductive sexual practices. It is true that if one wants to have a child, intercourse is one of the best means. But sex research has shown that if female sexual pleasure is the aim then intercourse is a poor choice, since masturbation and lesbian sex are both much more effective. (Shere Hite for example found that only 30 percent of a large sample of women regularly achieved orgasm from intercourse, while 99 percent of the women could easily achieve orgasm by masturbating.[3]) Men, for their part, often prefer fellatio to intercourse.

This sex research ought to have demolished once and for all the myth that sexual pleasure is maximized by intercourse. And the increasing availability of birth control ought also to have helped break the bond between sex and reproduction. But people still cling to the theory that the vagina is women's "real" sex organ and the "natural" receptacle for the penis and for sperm.

Why is this?

Well, perhaps the sexual revolution happened a bit too fast for us all. Despite our experiments in sexual practices we still keep alive the notion of intercourse as the most "natural" kind of sex, providing ourselves with a fixed point or home to which we can return. It is genuinely unsettling to watch old ideas and values go out the window. We are more comfortable adding diversions and "desserts" (as *The Joy of Sex* calls them) to our sexual repertoire than questioning the underlying assumptions of a hierarchy of sexual acts that puts regular intercourse in the role of "main dish" and everything else in the role of hors d'oeuvre. It is very important to question the division of sexual acts into "basic" or "natural" and "frills." Only after we have shaken the foundations of the old edifice will we be able to look honestly at our own sexual desires and decide what really pleases us. *The Joy of Sex* approach appears very liberated, but the way sexual acts are classified suggests that one would not want to make a whole meal out of "just" oral sex or "just" anal intercourse. The equation of intercourse with the protein in a meal is simply an ideological construct. This argument for intercourse as the real thing is based on assumptions about penises and vaginas "fitting" together. If we used our imagination, we could as easily argue that other bodily parts fit together. Try it. It's a good exercise for the imagination. Indeed, if a woman has to be told she is "infantile" and "immature" if she doesn't experience intercourse as the most natural and pleasurable form of sex, or if her privileging of the vagina is achieved only after a lengthy process of indoctrination and internalization of what being an adult woman is all about, then one must wonder how well penises and vaginas do fit together. The tired clichés used to convince us that our sexuality can be reduced to the vagina (the "lock" or the "glove") and the vagina in turn to a place for the penis (the "key" or the "hand") reveal a crucial logical fallacy, a phallocentric fallacy. The lock was made so that a key would fit into it, and has no purpose in and of itself; ditto for gloves, which make no sense if considered apart from hands. But vaginas have all sorts of purposes such as allowing menstrual blood out, and most importantly giving birth to children—that have nothing to do with the phallus. One is tempted to understand the clichés about the vagina as nothing but male jealousy and defensiveness around female reproduction. Threatened by a vagina whose darkness and wetness frightens them and whose life-giving powers both scare and mystify them, men try to ignore the independent life of the vagina and reduce it to a mere container, box, or receptacle. This interpretation has been elaborated by many feminist theorists, but first and foremost by Simone de Beauvoir, who made a detailed study of the many myths and rituals that have as their common denominator an attempt to safeguard men against the elemental powers of women's sexual and reproductive activities. She writes:

> In all civilizations and still in our day woman inspires man with horror: it is the horror of his own carnal contingence, which he projects upon her. . . . On the day she can reproduce, woman becomes impure; and rigorous taboos surround the menstruating female. . . . The blood, indeed, does not make woman impure; it is rather a sign of her impurity. It concerns generation, it flows from the parts where the fetus develops. Through menstrual blood is expressed the horror inspired in man by woman's fecundity.[4]

De Beauvoir further reminds us that the matter-of-fact, proprietory statements made by men about the "rightness" of intercourse sometimes conceal a deep-rooted fear of the un-known, of the supernatural, and an anxiety that the vagina is the worst possible place in which a penis might find itself.

> Certain peoples imagine that there is a serpent in the vagina which would bite the husband just as the hymen is broken; some ascribe frightful powers to virginal blood, related to menstrual blood and likewise capable of ruining the man's vi-gor. Through such imagery is expressed the idea that the fem-inine principle has the more strength, is more menacing, when it is intact.[5]

Men's fear of intercourse can on the one hand be traced back to these mythological fears—which are not as outdated as they might seem and exist today in such popular images as the cas-trating bitch, nymphomaniac, nun and Queen of the Night. On the other hand they are also rooted in the very real fear of regressing to infancy and being literally swallowed up by the Mother and sucked back into the womb.[7] Without going into detail about these fears and anxieties we can certainly conclude that having intercourse is not, for men, the matter-of-fact state-ment of natural possession they may claim it to be. The por-nography industry may spend millions trying to convince men that sex is safe and fun and unproblematic, but the image of the *vagina dentata* dies hard.

It seems to me that the male fear and envy of women's sex-ual and reproductive power is taken to the level of mythical misogyny when its basis in fact is not recognized. There are real differences between men and women which can give rise to reasonable curiosity and even anxiety or jealousy. For in-stance, a father may envy his wife's ability to nurse their child. Or a man may wonder why women seem to have a more varied sexual response. These feelings are normal and need not give rise to fearful images of serpents hidden in vaginas. But they might if they are not acknowledged, if they are repressed. It is not sexual difference itself which causes dread of women. Rather, it is the repression of one's child-like curiosity or nor-mal wonder, coupled with the ideological attempt to assert male superiority in all areas, which produces the kind of ele-mental anxiety that Simone de Beauvoir describes.

Ever since Freud theorized that female childhood sexuality

was first polysexual and then clitoral, we have had reasons other than our own intuition for doubting that intercourse is the *summum bonum*. In Freud's account of femininity, it is never quite clear why girls give up both their happy oral sexuality and their active clitoral masturbation in order to exclusively eroticize the vagina as a passive receptacle for the phallic King. Freud merely states that the little girl is so overwhelmed at the sight of the large penis that her own tiny clitoris seems too pitiful to bother with. "Her self-love is mortified by the comparison with the boy's far superior equipment and in consequence she renounces her masturbatory satisfaction from her clitoris, repudiates her lover for her mother. . . ."[7] And she goes on to train herself to be a happy wife and mother. Far-fetched as the concept of penis envy is, it is even more farfetched that the girl would give up her autoerotic pleasures. Why should she? Even if the penis is larger than the clitoris, at least she has a clitoris and all the envy in the world is not going to get her a penis. And is she really a size fetishist?

Freud was keen on legitimizing passive, vaginal sexuality as woman's highest calling but could not produce a better model of how this sexuality develops. One has to wonder if the whole enterprise is not impossible. Physiological, psychological and empirical arguments can be employed to demonstrate that some or even most women do in fact like intercourse at least some of the time. But what can never be proved is that intercourse is *the* sexual act and the highest good. We know women do not experience orgasm very often if the only sex they engage in is intercourse. And theoretically, we can find no reason why girls and women would relinquish the manifold possibilities of their bodies in order to concentrate exclusively on passive, penis-vagina intercourse. (Not that intercourse *has* to be passive; but tradition equates vaginal sexuality with passivity.)

And yet, despite all the evidence gathered to prove that vaginal intercourse is not *the* privileged form of female sexuality, the myths and clichés live on practically undisturbed. People continue to think penises and vaginas are "made for each other," and if by chance they do other things with their respective penises or vaginas they regard it as kinky, going against nature or the norm.

In referring to Simone de Beauvoir we touched on some of

the possible reasons why the idea of the penis and vagina as the happy couple *par excellence* might be so impervious to both logic and experience. One of these reasons was that the vagina, both sexually and reproductively, is simply too powerful and so must be constantly conquered by being constantly coupled. The awesome fertility goddesses of past cultures have been tamed and trivialized. They have been reduced to Playboy bunnies whose sexual parts are described as "clits" and "boxes," cutesy words which empty women's sexuality of its real power and leave the phallus holding the power monopoly.

The myth of intercourse is also sustained by the idea that all eroticism depends in an essential way on *difference*, and specifically *genital difference*. Now, this idea is not necessarily patriarchal in its form and intent, for difference does not necessarily imply subordination. There can be amiable, egalitarian difference, which is presumably what fuels eroticism among enlightened heterosexuals.

The idea of difference as erotic is so common-sense and commonplace that we do not usually pause to criticize it. We merrily proceed to examine our own erotic attraction to individual X or type Y and come up with the "differences" that are significant. But we could just as well analyze our own attractions and non-attractions by reference to similarities.

Let me give an example. A friend of mine once said "I like men because they're so different!" So I envisaged her with a tall, muscular hunk with a masculine beard and a masculine personality. But when I met her lover he turned out to be neither tall nor muscular nor aggressive; rather he was androgynous both in physique and personality. So where was the big difference? (My friend, incidentally, also looks more androgynous than feminine.) Was the difference that he had a penis? But other men who were much more "different" than this guy also had penises, and my friend was not interested in them. Was it really difference that attracted her to him?

There are many criteria one could use to measure human differences: size, weight, skin colour, hair colour, race, language, age, intelligence, physical fitness, beliefs, talents, etc. If a heterosexual couple is composed of two individuals who are remarkably similar in for example their class backgrounds, interests, and ethnicity (as is usually the case), and who are different primarily in their gender, then one can not claim with any certainty that the key to their erotic attraction is difference. In their case gender difference has been eroticized, but so have their much more numerous non-gender similarities.

It is not my intention to argue for the intrinsic erotic appeal of similarity or difference. Some people can only get interested in partners who are basically similar to them, while others need sharp differences in order to have their erotic interest sparked. To each her own, as far as I'm concerned. The point is that I do not see any valid reason for privileging gender above all else, and then *assuming* that gender difference is essentially erotic while other differences are not. In ancient Athenian culture, for instance, adult men saw adult women primarily as reproductive partners and reserved their odes to eroticism for adolescent boys. There, age differences were eroticized as a matter of course, whereas the gender difference might or might not have been erotic.

By understanding eroticism as a force which pivots around sex and gender differences we separate the erotic realm from other aspects of human existence. Activities and relationships in which sex and gender are not major factors are perceived as non-erotic. Now, to some extent there is clearly something specific about erotic interaction that makes it distinct from the pleasure of working together with others, or of having shared family roots. However, to take this distinction for granted and to absolutize it is a mistake that reinforces certain philosophical beliefs that are simply myths. First, the separation of the erotic—as the sexual, the mysterious, the irrational, the dialectic of difference—from other aspects of human interaction fosters a view of the human self as essentially and eternally divided between Reason and Passion. Secondly, because eroticism is exiled beyond the pale of reason, the everyday life of rational interaction is de-eroticized. And finally, separating Reason from Passion constructs a realm of the instinctual to which women are largely confined.

Women have suffered from this ideological division of the passionate and the rational, as many feminists have noted and criticized. Because erotic play is thought to depend on sexual difference and on the contrast between reason and passion, erotic relations have been largely confined to relations between unequals. Reason and Passion as the male and female principles are not simply different. They are unequal within the hierarchy that prevails between them. On the other hand, relations among equals as "thinking persons" have been a priori de-eroticized, because they hinge not on difference but on a sameness in what the philosophers have called "the common light of reason." Western philosophers have argued that this commonality is the basis both of thinking itself and of democratic society. Most of them also believed women did not share fully in the light of reason and therefore could not enter into the world of politics or philosophy. But even those few who argued that women did indeed have the prerequisite rationality and personhood to enter into the realm of reason and be participants in the social contract still left untouched the basic division between the erotic and the rational. Even if women had an element of rationality, they still had to represent Mother Earth and the dark instincts. And much popular culture since the nineteenth century hinges on women's *internal* struggle between their personhood, as the desire for example to learn or succeed, and their womanhood. This struggle is often tragic because the claims of the feminine are considered to be contradictory to the claims of personhood.

Thus whether or not women were allowed some access to the realm of reason and public life, there was still a sharp separation between "human" interactions (based on male-defined equality among rational human beings as conceived on the male model) and erotic interactions based on sexual difference. The equality prevailing in the intellectual world and the marketplace was considered to be inherently non-erotic, even anti-erotic, while the unequal struggle between Reason and Passion was understood as inherently sexy. Women's confinement to the realm of the semi-rational went hand in hand with a desexualization of the world of men, politics, work, and culture. One of the reasons for this was the age-old desire to use Reason as a tool to dominate nature, subjugate the passions, and not coincidentally to put women, as those closest to Nature, in their place. But certainly another reason was that to admit sexuality and eroticism into the public world would have necessarily entailed recognizing homosexuality, or at the very least homoeroticism. Thus, insofar as men and women were defined as being divided by sexual difference and so fundamentally unequal, society could not afford to eroticize equality.

A further result of this has been to create a much larger gap than necessary between heterosexuality and homosexuality. Just as we have exaggerated the role of difference in heterosexual eroticism, so too have we exaggerated the role of similarity in homosexuality. A gay man does not necessarily eroticize only his partner's masculinity. And two lesbians might have certain commonalities in bodily parts and psychological traits, but can otherwise be as different as night and day. So my point is not so much that one has to "make room for" homosexuality as an eroticism of sameness, but more fundamentally to question the very separation of sameness and difference, and the process by which we overvalue difference when theorizing about sexual attraction.

Heterosexuality is too complicated and too unpredictable to be reduced to such a simple formula as "boy meets girl," "like meets unlike," "opposites attract." Men and women are clearly different, but their attraction to one another does not necessarily depend only on that difference. And in any case they are not *opposites*. Because there happen to be only two sexes, we absolutize this fact and assume that the two sexes are opposites. But why? What if there were three or four sexes created through some miracle of modern science? Or if we only had two senses instead of five, would we assume that those two—sight and hearing, let's say—were "opposites"? If I have two daughters, or a daughter and a son, are they opposites of one another?

Heterosexuality cannot be free until we stop thinking in terms of "opposites" that are "drawn" to one another. Men and women are not like iron filings and magnets, keys and locks, or any object in those functionalist and fatalistic metaphors that try to legitimize heterosexuality as the norm by presenting it as a fate imposed on us by Nature. Heterosexuality is not our fate. It is a *choice* that we can make—or, more accurately, it *would be* a choice if our society were more pluralistic and less rigid in its construction of sexual choices. After all, choice implies the existence of several valid options, and as long as we continue to see eroticism between the sexes as fated by some inevitable sexiness inherent in genital differences, we will have a rather impoverished experience of heterosexuality.

Even if we cannot individually transcend the naturalistic view we can still work towards a freer heterosexuality by resisting this dominant ideology and attempting to maximize the creative possibilities that do exist. One thing we could do is stop repeating the myth—which we do not really believe in anyway—that we are attracted to men "just because they are different." Our own experience tells us otherwise: we are attracted to particular men partly because their "maleness" fascinates us, but also because of certain commonalities that we share as human beings or as members of certain groups. After all, we are not attracted to *all* men (as would be the case if we were attracted to sexual difference itself). On this particular man we might find muscles and a beard sexy, but on some other man we might be repulsed by the same "differences." We are not the puppets of a Mother Nature that manipulates our desires in order to have our feminine vagina become the "receptacle" for the masculine penis. We are human beings with very complex reasons for our erotic preferences.

In all our erotic desires and activities there is an interplay of sameness and difference, of recognition and fascination, of familiarity and strangeness. Neither difference nor sameness are per se erotic; rather it is the playful movement of and between them which creates erotic exchange. A consistent eroticism of difference would exaggerate sexual difference into a pornographic scenario where the man with the biggest cock gets the woman with the biggest breasts. And a consistent eroticism of sameness would be equally unimaginative and homogenized, with everyone so equal that we would have no reason to be attracted to one person rather than another. Thus, what we need to work toward and begin imagining is an eroticism where sameness and difference are both eroticized and valued. This can help us to both break down the walls of the ego and recognize the other as our equal while maintaining the "admiration" for otherness and difference. Perhaps the most important thing to remember is that men and women were not made for heterosexuality, but rather heterosexuality exists for men and women.

MAKING CHANGES—OR TRYING TO

Last year the progressive American magazine *Mother Jones* published a long confessional article by a woman who appeared to be independent and self-assured, except that she was repeatedly drawn into relationships with the most stereotypical macho men one can imagine. She liked soldiers, tough guys who had fought in Vietnam and had repressed all tenderness they might have once had. The men were white, big, strong—and often violent. They drank too much, never exercised their brain cells, and generally lived up to the television image of life in the army. The author recognized that her attraction to such men contained an element of self-destructiveness, but she couldn't help herself. She not only had sex with them, but also relationships of the most unequal and degrading kind.

In publishing this story the editors were clearly trying to stir up controversy among their left-Yuppie readership which by and large believes in egalitarian and committed heterosexuality and sees John Wayne as completely passé. They succeeded in their aim, and various letters to the editor in subsequent issues expressed a range of highly emotional reactions. Some readers thought "there must be something wrong with that woman, she's such a masochist." The implication here is "I never have desires like that." Other people expressed discomfort with the confession but concluded that we should never pass judgement on other people's sexuality, so live and let live.

These two reactions to one woman's frank avowal of very politically incorrect and unfeminist desires are typical of current discussions about women's desire for men. The dogmatists try to explain away any desires that do not fit the egalitarian paradigm and ignore any evidence of power in their own relationships. Women then who are attracted to alcoholic soldiers must be "sick."

On the other hand, the sexual libertarian feminist camp (a small one, to be sure, since most libertarians are men) refuses to examine the dynamics of specific relationships. They say as long as the woman is consenting to the sexual activity or the relationship, let her do what she wants and don't get moralistic.

The libertarians have a point. Many discussions of sexuality begin and end with moralistic judgements that in no way help us understand what is going on. They succeed only in reassuring the judges that *their* desires are properly feminist. However, moralism is not the only avenue for discussing sexuality. The woman with a fatal passion for soldiers need not be labelled as a masochist. Rather, one can try to understand what exactly she is looking for in soldiers. By referring to both her social context—for example the American ideology of military masculinity—and her own psychological development—who were her parents? how did her sexuality develop?—we can try to understand how this woman's erotic preferences fit within the underlying patterns of her sexual and social life.

By choosing to make her love of soldiers into a problem to write about, this woman was already standing back and attempting to understand if and how she might change her sexual patterns. The caricatured masculinity of the men made it relatively easy to see her attraction for them as "a problem." But what if she had been attracted to middle-aged surgeons with large bank accounts? That would not make an interesting feature for *Mother Jones*, no matter how hard she tried to problematize her desire. "Fatal attraction to upper-class men almost ruined my life"; "Sordid passion for stockbrokers"; "Why do Yuppies turn her on?" No, these just would not wash as headlines. Yet there is no reason why a passion for lawyers or stockbrokers could not be as fatal to a woman's sense of confidence and self-worth as an attraction to boxers, football players or soldiers. Being treated as an investment is not necessarily better than being treated as war booty, though on the surface it may appear more civilized.

The point here is that if we are going to undertake the process of making changes we have to begin by deciding what it is we want to change. The woman in *Mother Jones* was not clear whether she thought the problem was that many of her men had been either alcoholic or violent or both, or if the issue was her fascination with the army. If the latter, she might have tried joining the army herself to get over her lingering fascination. If the former, she would have had to analyze her history of and feelings about domestic violence and alcohol. Alternatively, she could have chosen to analyze her experiences not as bizarre occurrences, but as exaggerated versions of normal feminine behaviour.

Many people are prevented from regarding certain aspects of their lives as problems because these are portrayed ideologically as normal and "natural." Women who are strongly committed to feminism sometimes have the opposite reaction. Not only do they try to analyze gender roles in their own relationships, but they feel vaguely guilty about being attracted to men at all. Their feminism has made them sharply aware of how male power is used, abused and reproduced in personal relationships, to the point where they despair of ever achieving equality. They begin to question their attachment to men and wonder if it is really men's bodies they desire, or if they are merely addicted to their power.

Experiencing feminism and heterosexuality as contradictory, many women have opted for a separation between their public life—as strong feminists, as women who work with other women—and their personal life. A feminist might be very attached to a man who is not without his faults but is generally pro-feminist, and yet feel vaguely embarrassed by her love for him. I have on occasion seen women appear at a party or public event and completely ignore the man they live with; once I practically had to force a woman I had worked with for years to introduce me to the man whom I knew was her partner.

British feminist Angela Hamblin comments on this situation:

> Over the past decade an increasing number of feminist women have been involved in transforming the basis upon which we are prepared to share our sexuality with men. It has been, for the most part, a very private struggle. . . . The net result has been that, as heterosexual feminists, we have found ourselves isolated . . . , thrown back into defining our relationships with men as belonging to the 'personal' sphere of our lives, cut off from our political concerns.[8]

In many women's groups, and especially those that include lesbians, there is often collusion in pretending that personal relationships with men either do not exist or are unimportant. We are strong women, after all, and we do not want to encourage the idea that women are defined by their relations to men. And sometimes lesbians contribute to heterosexual guilt by giving the impression that women's heterosexuality is a weakness, a chink in their feminist armour. However, I do not know any lesbian feminists who really believe heterosexuality is per se an unfeminist state of being. Many of the social relations that tend to accompany heterosexuality are indeed problematic, but these structural problems do not cast any aspersions on women's sexual passion for men. It is true that many feminists, and not only lesbians, consider constant references to one's husband or boyfriend tedious and in poor political taste. But when a woman is clearly in sexual heaven, there is no reason for suppressing her passion.

Being passionate about a man is not the same as being dependent on him. The joy one feels when a sexual relationship is going well should be shared among women; discussions of men need not be reserved for when things are going badly and we need support from our sisters. Clearly, tact is needed so as not to make single women feel left out or lesbians feel that their relationships do not count. But it is crucial to our collective growth that we take risks and share the happiness our bodies feel. As feminists we might be skeptical about women who appear to need male approval for their very survival. But precisely for this reason we should be happy when women desire men without needing them.

We need to learn to talk about our sexual desires. When women converse with one another they usually have an agenda item labelled "relationships." Yet this is not at all the same thing as talking about sex. First, while not all sex takes place within relationships, our conventions make it extremely difficult to share sexual experiences of the more casual variety. Secondly, even within a relationship we tend to remain silent about its sexual component. This is not surprising, given that we often cannot even talk about sex with our lovers.

What would happen if we were to make sex a regular item in our conversations, just as we discuss work and politics?

Most discussions in which I have participated deal with sex only in an oblique manner. For instance, someone might broach the topic of contraception and end up revealing a few things about her sexual life by way of a scientific discussion of diaphragms. Or someone confides in a friend that she is afraid she might have gotten herpes from sleeping with X or Y. But we never phone up a friend and say, "Let me tell you about this great sexual experience I just had." We would feel foolish, as if we were jocks telling each other locker room stories.

However, sharing our sexual feelings, our frustrations, moments of ecstasy and our secret desires, is a necessary part of being feminists together. We believe "the personal is the political," and what could be more personal than sex?

One reason for our collective silence might be precisely that we have taken that slogan too much to heart, and are worried that our sexual practices might be found "politically incorrect." But I think feminism has matured considerably on this question. At one point there were vehement denunciations of male penetration as inherently sadistic and anti-woman, but I think few would make this kind of judgement today. And for every one dogmatic comment, there are many, many more women who are non-judgemental and respond by exchanging ideas and feelings.

I suspect that the biggest barrier to talking about sex is not so much the fear of others' reactions as the fear that we ourselves will not like what we see. Many of the women interviewed by Angela Hamblin were forced to admit that they had for some time acquiesced to sexual practices that demeaned them. One woman said:

> I've felt pressured into sex—by persuasion, by arguments, by insults and by force. I had a fairly long term relationship with a man who refused to have sex on any terms but his own which meant that I was constantly pressurized into sexual intercourse. . . . He gave me no space for developing my own sexuality.[9]

The woman speaking is clearly angry at the man, but she is equally angry at herself for not *taking* more space. She states she was often insulted and forced into sex, and adds that this was in a "fairly long relationship," a qualification which adds to her self-blame. She probably resisted sex on occasion, but instead of highlighting her resistance she emphasizes her weakness. By portraying herself as victim, she performs the feminist equivalent of confessing one's sins. And as we discussed earlier, she then anticipates pity and forgiveness from her feminist readership.

◆

It is very difficult indeed to avoid moral judgements, especially of oneself, and to find ways to describe unpleasant experiences without relying on the confessional model. And it is especially difficult to be straightforward when we feel ambivalent about our own attraction to men and have difficulty in distinguishing passion from dependence, and the sexual aspect of heterosexuality from its social and political aspects. "Giving in" sexually to a man has often meant giving in to all of patriarchy; letting oneself be seduced has often meant letting a man believe he has power over *all* women. Thus, we feel a particular responsibility for resisting male power, and if we don't resist we feel we have let down our sisters.

Even though there is a great deal of truth in these statements, we simply cannot bear the whole weight of patriarchy (or of feminism) on our individual shoulders. We have to be kinder to ourselves, and not feel that because we gave in to a man, or faked an orgasm, that feminism suffers a serious setback. And when we begin to talk about sex, we must do so with self-respect, giving ourselves the same kind of affection and understanding that we would give other women. We have all at various times fallen into roles or let a man get away with too much. But we cannot be superwomen, and we cannot singlehandedly bring about a non-sexist social system. We can be annoyed with ourselves for having gone along with a male-defined sexual scenario, or for having endured in a relationship we knew was unequal and not respectful of us. But we do not have to feel *ashamed* of anything we have ever done. Shame and guilt do not bring about changes in our patterns of behaviour, rather we tend to repeat those very acts that make us feel guilt or shame.

A frank acceptance of ourselves as we are would go a long way in preparing ourselves to speak with one another and help each other in our hitherto private sexual struggles. We can learn to take a critical distance from our own acts, and even learn to laugh at ourselves for doing stereotypical things. But we should never feel that we have to get down on our knees and declare ourselves unworthy of our own feminist ideals.

Last year I was out of town for a week at a conference. The second night I was there I stayed up late with a few people, talking about the prospects for socialism in Latin America and other topics of common interest. There was a man present, a Latin American who had originally struck me as a typical ladies' man. But as we drank together I saw that he was someone clearly fuelled by a passionate revolutionary conviction. Eventually everybody went to bed except for this man, another woman and myself. The man (I will call him Daniel) at one point stood up, went around behind my chair and put his hand on the back of my neck. I should have felt patronized, but I felt horny instead. The other woman was signalling her availability by subtle but unmistakable signs, and as I watched her I decided that *I* wanted to sleep with Daniel that night. (I could feel my sexual interest being heightened by the presence of competition, which was an odd, unfamiliar feeling.) At the same time I did not want to make a fool of myself by coming on to him too strongly, so I tried to walk a fine line between interest and disinterest, responding to his looks but not too eagerly.

After a while it became clear to the other woman that she had "lost," and she graciously retired. Left alone with Daniel, I wondered if I really wanted to go through with it. I barely knew him, and we had to work together for the rest of the week. But after one more look from his black eyes, I threw caution to the wind. He had had more than one drink too many, and he suggested we go out for a walk, which I thought was a good idea since it would help sober him up. We went out into the still and warm tropical night. Soon enough we were kissing passionately. We went back to our hotel, went to his room, and I stood quietly (like a good mistress, I thought with a smile) as he convinced his roommate—who was fast asleep—to wake up, get up and go somewhere else. He did, sailing past without looking at me. I felt a bit ridiculous, but put my embarrassment firmly out of my mind.

Finally, the door was closed, and we went to bed without many preliminaries. He showed some concern for birth control, which surprised me agreeably; but once we had passed that hurdle he proceeded to take control and define the sexual scenario according to his ideas of how good sex ought to happen. I was somewhat startled—I am much more used to tentativeness and mutual hesitancy than to the kind of self-assuredness he was showing—but at the same time there was something decidedly pleasant about it. Although he assumed the role of director, he was not selfish in demanding pleasure, and in fact we probably spent more time on my pleasures than on his, insofar as one can make that distinction. From fairly conventional intercourse we progressed to various other possibilities, and my passion seemed to multiply. When he said to me, fairly imperiously, "turn over," I did so not just willingly but with a passion that matched his own. As the sun came up, I felt—my body felt—unspeakably happy.

I had a definite sense of having done something that was wrong in the eyes of both traditionalists and feminists. I had competed with another woman for a man's sexual favours, which meant not only that I was unsisterly but also that I was unnecessarily boosting the man's ego. Then I let him find us a place to make love; then I let him take control of sex itself. He was not hesitant to voice his desires, while I remained mostly silent. Last but not least, he was about fifteen years older than me, married, and obviously seeking a younger woman for exclusively sexual purposes. And he was possibly on his way to alcoholism.

Not a great balance sheet, on the whole. And yet, I knew precisely what was going on, had no illusions about him, and chose to go ahead anyway and enjoy it as much as possible. The kind of sex we had, indicated that any attempt at an ongoing affair was doomed—he probably regarded "his" women as property—but as a spontaneous one-night stand with no consequences it was just fine. Thus, I disregarded not only what other people might think but also what I might think the next day. If I had been in Toronto I probably would never have been so bold, but I figured nobody I knew had to know.

Now, I am by no means advocating casual sex with agreeable but sexist middle-aged men as any kind of recipe for anything. By and large, good sex with men tends to take place within a relationship, where there is time for men to learn our rhythms and time for us to open up and trust men. And in any case, good sex does not fulfil our needs for affection and sympathy which clearly cannot be met by men we meet casually.

The point is, however, that sometimes we can manage to get pleasure in unlikely circumstances, and we need to keep an open mind for the unexpected. The world we live in is not designed to further women's bodily pleasures, and even when we find an opportunity for sexual pleasure the social context may be all wrong. Under these circumstances, we cannot be too hard on ourselves or others for trying to make the best out of a basically unfavourable situation.

Occasionally though we sometimes manage to gain a glimpse of a kind of sex between men and women that is devoted purely to mutual pleasure, and in which social relations of power are suspended. Some and perhaps most women will find that glimpse only in long-term relationships where there has been a long process of mutual adjustment and of *creating* equality. Other women might be unable to find a companion who is willing to engage in that process, or they might for various reasons choose not to take up this kind of long-term struggle. In these latter cases, the women in question will have to find ways to express their heterosexuality outside the context of a couple.

It would be nice to be able to finish this chapter with an ode to diversity, enumerating the variety of ways women can explore their passion for men and find satisfaction. However this would be unrealistic without considering today's problem of scarcity, which plagues heterosexual women and especially feminists.

THE SCARCITY PROBLEM

There is no doubt that one of the main barriers to the sexual liberation of heterosexual women is the scarcity of suitable men. Women in their mid-thirties or beyond find that they do not meet many non-sexist, good-looking, interesting men in the course of their daily lives. And if they do, as a friend of mine complained, "all the nice ones are taken."

The scarcity is not just one of sexual opportunities. Our society is organized in such a way that uncoupled heterosexual women are deprived of many other things: companionship on weekends, someone to tell one's worries to or borrow money from, someone to go on holidays with. There is a great deal of truth in the cliché that the world moves in couples. When you are not in a couple, your social life suffers as much or more than your sexual life. If you feel like going out for dinner, you have to make plans to go out with a friend, but it is difficult to find a pleasant partner for spontaneous outings. You may also get fewer invitations to dinner parties, and when you get invitations from coupled friends you might feel like an awkward fifth wheel.

And, no matter how independent and assertive we are, it is difficult to escape the belief that women's attractiveness is defined by the sexual marketplace. It is difficult to maintain a sense of ourselves as desirable and attractive if we do not succeed in the coupling game. The objective conditions are stacked against us, especially if we are past our mid-thirties, because most men prefer a cute twenty-one-year-old to a self-assured feminist of thirty-eight. Statistically then our chances of becoming involved with a man are slim. Slimmer still is the chance of finding a man who is willing to challenge his own sexism in a relationship. Even if we realize it is not our fault that relationships are difficult to come by, we tend to compare ourselves unfavourably with those women friends who are part of a couple. We also sometimes idealize their relationships, not realizing that they too have to make compromises and put up with less than perfect situations.

The scarcity problem means that once we are in a relationship, we will go a long way to maintain it, to some extent by compromising our principles. If the alternative to man X is loneliness, we might put up with all kinds of irritating habits that we would not tolerate in a female roommate. The guy in question may not be perfect, but he has the virtue of Mount Everest in simply being there. This reminds me of what a friend calls "the last man in the world syndrome," a syndrome which can afflict women at a surprisingly young age.

It is easy to diagnose the over-dependence of a woman who is suffering from this syndrome, but much more difficult to suggest ways for her to gain more control over the relationship. By the time we get to be around forty, never mind fifty, there is in fact a good chance that any particular man we have an affair with will be the last chance for a committed relationship. *We* know that aging does not have to be ugly and lonely, but the rest of the world does not seem to have caught on yet. This can put much undue pressure on a relationship, and can heighten the tendency to jealousy.

Another aspect of the scarcity problem is that without a regular partner one faces the dilemma of choosing between celibacy or finding occasional sexual partners. The latter alternative takes quite a bit of energy, and produces results unsatisfying at even a purely sexual level. Many women go through a stage of trying to have casual affairs with men they do not know well, only to find that either they get too emotionally involved for their own good, or regret their decision upon discovering that the men in question are completely objectionable.

When I was an undergraduate I went through just such a stage for a couple of years. I would have to admit that my goal—fun, casual, uncomplicated sex with a basically decent guy—was achieved only on rare occasions. One or two guys turned out to be nothing short of creeps, and sleeping together revealed more about them than I ever wanted to know. Another man could not seem to cope with easy-going, friendly sex, and stopped acknowledging me as a friend or even a co-worker after we had had sex a couple of times. And one rather bizarre man (who, incidentally, turned out to be impotent) decided to fall in love with me. I was obliged to take to the hills. Over the course of two or three years only a couple of men "worked out." The sex was all right, there were no emotional bills to pay afterward, and the sex was integrated into a more or less casual friendship.

Thus, when I fell in love with a man who was intelligent, handsome, and not afraid of his own emotions, I was not at all reluctant to settle down and eventually get married. Strict monogamy was not part of the agreement, but I had no fear that I would find it difficult to maintain a basic loyalty and commitment to this man. I had never before even come close to falling in love, and I had no reason to think another wonderful man would suddenly materialize. I did not want to completely give up my right to sleep with others (and neither did he), but I doubted I would exercise that option very often.

Casual sex is for women so fraught with pitfalls that it is understandable so many uncoupled women end up leading a basically celibate life. However, I still feel it is important not to give up completely on sex outside of relationships. One may have to be careful about the risks, but if we stop trying altogether we are perpetuating the old system whereby women's sexual pleasure is only allowed within a committed relationship. This is not to say there are not good reasons for some women to choose celibacy. As I see it, celibacy is a positive choice to opt out of the sexual game altogether and stop looking for partners for that purpose. My point is addressed not to women who are celibate by choice but to those who are looking for sexual partners. For these women, problems can arise if one is too finicky or too insistent on tying up all loose ends before going to bed with someone. After a long period of being celibate and spending a lot of time and energy planning how to acquire a relationship, we may have trouble being relaxed in an affair. We may invest it with all kinds of significance that it does not intrinsically have, and handicap ourselves by falling into the "last man in the world" syndrome.

We are not going to see, in our lifetime, the emergence of a whole new generation of men our age who are both suitable and interested in relationships. That is the sad but true reality. So we might as well experiment with other approaches to sex, without harbouring many illusions about the potential of casual affairs. We can plan many things about our lives but we cannot plan its sexual aspect with any certainty. Among the heterosexual women I know, the ones who seem to be the happiest are those who keep an open mind about sexual partners and sexual pleasure in general, but who do not depend too much on either their partner or men in general. The unhappiest women are those who set themselves such artificial deadlines and tests as, "If I don't get a man by the time I'm forty, that's it," or "If this relationship fails, then I am no good."

That kind of thinking can ruin not just one's single life but even a good relationship.

Furthermore, we have to train ourselves to distinguish sexual desire from emotional needs. This is not always easy to do. We have to accept that we will continue to need our friends for emotional support and good talks even if and when we become involved with a man. And we have to accept that a non-sexual friendship with a man or woman may in the end be more important to our emotional well-being, and more deserving of our energy and commitment, than some sexual relationships. If we keep our expectations realistic, and avoid treating a partner as the last man in the world (even if we think he might be!), we will be more relaxed and better able to survive ups and downs and even failures. By diversifying our emotional investments—and I apologize for the stock-market analogy—we will not be as vulnerable to sudden disaster.

THE CRISIS IN HETEROSEXUALITY

When we are feeling down about a relationship or about the absence of one, it might be useful to reflect on the fact that the troubles we are experiencing are not due simply to our own personal crises but rather to the historical crisis of heterosexuality. Many of the traditional norms that helped to form couples and keep them together in previous decades are visibly crumbling. But we are still the products of our childhoods, and have certain emotional needs and expectations which cannot easily be met in today's world. Most of us were brought up in relatively conventional nuclear families, and even those who were not are deeply affected by the ideology that reigned more or less unchallenged. However, most of us will not spend the rest of our lives in such units. As both creatures of our upbringing and adults in the post-sexual revolution world, we have contradictory needs and wishes. We want lifelong security, but we also want complete autonomy. We have a certain sense of our rights and responsibilities in relationships, but we also believe freedom is important and that people have to grow in their own ways. These beliefs being contradictory, it is small wonder that we often feel confused.

Apart from the general, cross-gender crisis in sexual and

family life,* women who have come to believe in the need for women's independence face an additional set of problems and contradictions. We will not settle for a conventional relationship where the man makes the major decisions and we merely shake our heads once in a while in the knowledge that "boys will be boys." We expect a great deal from men, because we ourselves have gone through major changes. But even the men who have an intellectual commitment to equality do not find it easy to break age-old patterns which, after all, were there precisely in order to guarantee a comfortable life for them. This means there is always a potential for conflict, and knowing this can bring us to something close to despair. After all, nobody really wants to struggle constantly in the house, in the bedroom, in the kitchen, over the kids and over the housework. We would like to leave our struggles against patriarchy outside our door and come home to a loving partner. And yet we cannot, even if we would like to, even if we try to ignore problems. Once we have been transformed by the impact of feminism we carry that critical consciousness everywhere we go, and cannot turn it off at will. Although we can on occasion suspend our feminist judgement and "let something go by," we cannot pretend to ourselves that we could be happy in a stifling relationship.

Perhaps we should try to look at the situation differently, by being amazed and surprised that there *are* some relationships that work. It is remarkable that some men have taken up the challenge of building sexual and social relationships that do not automatically further male interests. It is surprising that so many people have left the old patterns behind and are trying to build their lives by improvising with the few indications that we can gather from our own lives, our beliefs, and the experiences of others. Because it is all too easy to find fault with ourselves—we have to take stock of the positive changes we *have* made.

And again, our personal struggles have to be put in the context of a collective struggle by millions of women around the world to question old norms and create the conditions for a different kind of life. We ourselves may be caught in the middle, in the stage that comes after the destruction of the old but

*See the last chapter for more on the ethics of sexuality.

before the reconstruction. We may feel depressed about our own personal prospects. But when changes are made by one woman or one couple somewhere, these changes are not just their own, but contribute to the creation of new foundations for us all. In a very real sense we are in the midst of a revolutionary situation, and nobody said it was easy or fun to be caught in a revolution. Some of us will manage to create relatively happy and egalitarian relationships with men; some of us will have a mixed bag of successes and failures; some of us will end up relating to men primarily in non-sexual ways. But we are all in it together. We should avoid the tendency to compete with one another and evaluate wins and losses in the heterosexual sweepstakes. It is necessary to retain a political, historical sense of the importance of the process in which we are collectively involved. And we can realistically hope that because of the struggles we have gone through, our daughters and sons will start their sexual lives with fewer handicaps than we had.

◆

CHAPTER THREE

LESBIANISM: A COUNTRY THAT HAS NO LANGUAGE

THE FOLLOWING SCENE is from Radclyffe Hall's classic novel of lesbian love, *The Well of Loneliness*. It takes place between the heroine, Stephen, and her mother, just after the mother finds out that Stephen has been sending passionate love letters to another woman. This is the mother speaking:

> I would rather see you dead at my feet than standing before me with that thing upon you—this unspeakable outrage that you call love in that letter which you don't deny having written. In that letter you say things that may only be said between man and woman, and coming from you they are vile and filthy words of corruption—against nature, against God who created nature . . . I ask myself what I have ever done to be dragged down into the depths by my daughter . . . I have loved —do you hear? I have loved your father, and your father loved me. That was *love*.

Then the daughter answers:

> As my father loved you, I loved. As a man loves a woman, that was how I loved—protectively, like my father. I wanted to give all that I had in me to give . . . All my life I've never felt like a woman, and you know it—you say that you've always disliked me, that you've always felt a strange physical repulsion . . . but what I will never forgive is your daring to try to make me ashamed of my love. I'm not ashamed of it, there's no shame in it.[1]

Today, a young lesbian confronting her mother is not likely to say she "had never felt like a woman" since our concepts of womanhood are not as rigid as they were in 1928. A young lesbian would not assume that if she loved women "protectively" she was necessarily assuming the male role. However the conversation still has much contemporary relevance. Many mothers and fathers still disparage their lesbian daughters' love. They might not bring God and nature into the discussion (although they often do, even when they are not strong believers in either) but they generally think lesbian love is a tragic and low passion compared to the lofty emotional and moral heights of married heterosexuality.

Many people who claim to be tolerant and are proud of themselves for being polite to a gay person at work, go into a frenzy if someone within their own family is discovered to be gay. "I've nothing against lesbians, but I wouldn't want my daughter to marry one" is a common belief among liberal heterosexuals in the 1980s.

Popular wisdom suggests two alternative explanations for the existence of lesbians. One is that sometimes one's genes get screwed up along the line, and so lesbians are "born that way." The other explanation is that some early trauma such as incest causes girls to become frightened of men and turn to other women for love. And popular wisdom also claims that many women who think of themselves as lesbians aren't really so. They are just "going through a phase" because some man treated them badly, or they are innocent darlings seduced by an older wicked woman. The same person will tell you that if you had good heterosexual relationships and then became a lesbian, you're not a real lesbian because you like men. But if you haven't had heterosexual relations then you can't possibly know that you would not enjoy them, so you are not a real lesbian either. It would seem our society has a lot invested in denying the possibility of the existence of lesbianism as a positive choice.

The genes theory is now discredited by scientists. It could never account anyway for the large numbers of women who are heterosexual for many years and then become lesbians; or for women who are lesbians for years and then become heterosexual. The first case could be "explained" by arguing that conditioning led a woman to heterosexuality before she discovered her "true" desires, but the second case could not be explained at all.

The trauma theory is equally unsubstantiated. Canadian statistics suggest that one out of four girls suffers some form of sexual abuse from men in her childhood or adolescence. But most of those girls grow up to be heterosexual, while many lesbian women do not have any history of sexual abuse.

The point is however that the very question "What causes lesbianism?" is incorrectly posed. It assumes that lesbianism is like taking a wrong turn on the highway. If only she could discover where the wrong turn was taken, she could go back and retrace her steps. But this assumes that there is *one* correct route set out on the map of sexual development. We cannot discuss sexual attraction between women and understand its "causes" without a general theory of sexual development. The model which assumes that girls will grow up to be heterosexual in the same way that acorns grow into oak trees labels lesbianism from the outset as pathological. The model is based on prejudices and a profound heterosexual bias.

Lesbianism is not a disease. It is not even a natural physiological or psychological condition. It is a complex social fact. Sex between women may have taken place for thousands of years, but the formation of a distinct lesbian identity—perceived as inherent, persisting even in the absence of sexual activity—is a relatively recent event. We cannot understand the position of lesbians in today's society without knowing some of the history of when and how this distinct sexual identity was formed.

A BIT OF HISTORY

Historian Lillian Faderman has pointed out in her groundbreaking book *Surpassing the Love of Men: Romantic Friendships and Love Between Women*[2] that both sex and love between women were part of European and American culture from the sixteenth to the nineteenth centuries, while strictly speaking there were no lesbians until the turn of the twentieth century.

Sexual activity between women was the object of the voyeuristic fascination of decadent French poets who fantasized about kinky "Sapphists." Indeed there may have been prostitutes or other women who engaged in same-sex sexual activity. However, this sexual activity was not envisaged as a real alternative to the heterosexual life. It was an exotic spice to relieve the sexual boredom of courtesans or the men who orchestrated these proto-pornographic encounters. It seems this kind of sexual activity was rare and confined to the social fringes.

On the other hand, strong love between women was both common and respectable. The "romantic friendship" of the late eighteenth and nineteenth centuries was an accepted feature of a social life that did not assume the women involved were in any way deviant or anti-heterosexual. Historian Carroll Smith-Rosenberg was the first to uncover a whole tradition of such long-lasting bonds of love between American women in the nineteenth century. She discovered many cases of women friends who would even displace the husband from the marital bed when visiting one another.[3] Sometimes the women did not marry and lived together as a couple, an arrangement known as a "Boston marriage." This was more common in the late nineteenth century, and only in urban settings since pioneer women tended to marry.

Faderman suggests that these passionate and sensual relationships that involved all the earmarks of passionate love, as we can see in surviving letters and other documents, were not usually based on genital sexual contact. The women might have slept in the same bed, hugged and kissed each other, and experienced all the signs of falling in love, but they probably did not think of their kisses or their racing pulses as indicators of a specifically genital desire. After all, in this era women were supposed to have only emotional desires, and there is evidence to show that most if not all women internalized this idea. For most, "sex" probably meant less than satisfying contact with overbearing husbands, or simply reproduction. When "in love" with another woman, they would not associate those feelings with either reproduction or with "base" desires.

Faderman tells of an interesting case which illustrates the disjunction between sex and love. It involved two Scottish schoolmistresses in the early nineteenth century who were brought to court by the family of one of their pupils on charges of committing "unnatural" acts with each other. The pupil was half English and half East Indian, and she claimed to have heard the two schoolmistresses make peculiar noises while in bed together at night. Now, the interesting point is that the passionate letters the two women had written to one another were introduced as evidence by the *defense* lawyers, not the prosecution. The lawyers argued that two women capable of such lofty feelings, such Christian devotion to one another, could not possibly stoop to the kind of dirty behaviour English gentlemen thought took place only in French brothels. It was also suggested that the student had an overactive sexual imagination due to her Indian parentage.

The lawyers' reasoning was similar to that of Queen Victoria when in 1885 she refused to sign a law that would have made lesbianism illegal, on the grounds that no British woman could possibly entertain such thoughts. Perhaps she was afraid that if a law banning lesbianism existed, Christian British women would get ideas.

The point is that women could and did love each other and without being considered members of an outcast group marked by abnormality and perversion. Romantic friendships confirmed the popular belief that women were by nature emotional, and so they were not regarded as a threat to either male authority or the institution of heterosexuality.

It was only after the 1880s that love between women began to be regarded with suspicion and investigated for signs of perversion. Havelock Ellis in Britain, Richard von Krafft-Ebing in Germany, and other doctors and scientists began to take an interest in classifying human sexual behaviour according to "types." They established criteria for distinguishing the various types, especially the normal and the abnormal. Some of these types were the fetishist, the sado-masochist and the necrophiliac. But foremost among the abnormal sexual types was the "invert" or homosexual.

The sexologists did not see homosexual activity as a moral lapse that anyone might fall into. Rather, they saw it as the visible manifestation of a congenital drive found among individuals of a certain type. Some sexologists tried to distinguish between homosexuality or "inversion" that was the result of inborn pathological sexual drives, and activity that was merely perverse. They tried therefore to separate the "true invert" from those who might indulge in abnormal sexual behaviour without necessarily being abnormal themselves. It was often argued that "true inverts" could not help being what they were, and thus should be treated with understanding and tolerance as long as they did not corrupt "normal" boys or girls.

For women, the impact of the new sexology was mixed. On the one hand, women who felt sexual urges toward other women could now put a name to their feelings, and argue, as did Radclyffe Hall's heroine, that they could not help being what they were, and hence need not be ashamed. But on the other hand, the new homosexual identity was not on par with heterosexuality. To be a lesbian was to be abnormal, and as the heroine of *The Well of Loneliness* also said, to be something other than a real woman. By adopting the sexologists' categories one might achieve inner peace knowing that one's feelings and experiences had a name and were shared by other women. However, one could never be at peace with the world since lesbianism was so stigmatized that even speaking about it was not allowed.

The new lesbian identity was a mixed blessing. Lesbians might be able to name and recognize themselves, but for this advantage they paid the price of being marked as abnormal personality types, as "masculine" women. Women who "felt masculine" and rejected femininity would thus scrutinize themselves for signs of incipient lesbianism, while women who loved other women would scrutinize their childhood for signs of rebellion against femininity. Radclyffe Hall's heroine typically grew up thinking she was a boy in disguise (her father helped things along by naming her Stephen), and the reader makes the connection between Stephen's fondness for horseback riding and other sports and her sexual perversion. Thus the lesbian was not just a sexual type, but a social type whose identity reached far beyond the sphere of sex.

The emergence of a lesbian identity was facilitated not only by the new sexology but also by the social changes affecting middle-class urban women in the late nineteenth century. Women were entering universities and the professions, and it became possible for middle-class women to earn their own living and even have a career. Clearly, without these material conditions it would have been impossible for women, whatever their sexual urges, to build lives that were relatively independent not only of husbands but of families in general. The "new women" of the turn of the century tended to band together and feel like outcasts in male-dominated professions and universities, thus increasing the possibilities for lesbian-ism.[4]

The formation of this outcast group of lesbians out of different elements that had existed in relative isolation (romantic friendship, sexual attraction between women, feminist desires for independence) did not only affect the women who appropriated the label "lesbian" for themselves. The homosexual identity was formed at the same time as, and in contrast to, the equally new identity of heterosexuality. Whereas during the nineteenth century womanhood had been defined primarily by motherhood, and not by sexual drives or desires, the early twentieth century saw an increasing heterosexualization of womanhood. The new British and American feminists of the 1920s and 1930s post-suffrage era rejected the asexuality of the earlier feminists and affirmed women's (hetero)sexuality as an important facet of women's liberation.[5] They were strongly influenced by sexology and by the theories of Freud and other psychological experts, which emphasized sexual fulfilment. They also became active in birth control campaigns in order to allow the separation of sex and reproduction to become a reality. Women like Margaret Sanger in the United States, and Rebecca West and Dora Russell in Britain promoted a new concept of womanhood which for the first time in the history of feminism included women's right to sexual fulfilment.

As heterosexuality and homosexuality became more distinct from each other and more significant as social and sexual entities, many journalists and popularizers of science launched a campaign to warn the public about the dangers of school crushes and same-sex affection of any kind. Whereas in the past coeducation was rejected as immoral, in the 1920s in Britain, the United States and Canada aspersions began to be cast on the moral character of all-girl or all-boy institutions. The sudden popularity of the new ideas about the dangers of homosexuality was very closely related to the "back-to-the-family," anti-feminist reaction experienced in many countries after World War I. In the United States women who had worked in the war effort and had just obtained the right to vote were now supposed to help create a new, suburban America where men were breadwinners and women were housewives. The lively socialist movement that had flourished in the 1910-1918 period was crushed in the "Red Scare" that followed the Russian Revolution. Radical immigrants such as Russian born anarchist feminist Emma Goldman were deported to their countries of origin, and loans were given to male workers to enable them to purchase homes and thus gain a stake in the post-war American dream.

As historian Dolores Hayden explains in *The Grand Domestic Revolution*, anti-communism, anti-feminism, and the glorification of the nuclear family all went hand in hand in the strategies of American business and government leaders.[6] The non-revolutionary, contented working-class family of the 1920s was supposed to be held together not only by the newly acquired home but also by the pleasures of sex. As social historian Linda Gordon puts it, "the mass culture of the 1920s told women to learn to grip and manipulate their husband's interest through their attractiveness. In Middletown people went to films and read articles with titles like 'Married Flirt' and 'How to Keep the Thrill in Marriage'."[7]

The intensification of heterosexuality led to a higher visibility of women who did not fit the bill. While women's sexuality had been ignored or deemed non-existent, lesbians and heterosexual women had little opportunity to define themselves as such and perceive themselves as different from one another. But when marriage began to be seen as primarily for sex and secondarily for reproduction, then the "true love" of man and woman, as the mother in *The Well of Loneliness* said, looked very different from the perverted love of two women. Romantic friendships either vanished or became tarred with the brush of perversion. Womanhood, previously identified with mothering and nurturing, now came to be defined by heterosexuality.

MAKING HETEROSEXUALITY COMPULSORY

With women increasingly defined and evaluated according to their heterosexual market value, and with marriage viewed neither as an economic partnership nor a parenting project but as a glorious romance, the stage was set for the social institution that had come to be known as "compulsory heterosexuality."[8] This institution is not located in any downtown skyscraper or in any government department, but it is so pervasive in today's society that it resembles the proverbial water of which fish are unaware.

Sexism creates femininity and masculinity as we know them, since our gendered egos are constituted by psychosocial conditioning. Compulsory heterosexuality refers to the ideology and social practice that pushes properly gendered women and men into couples and makes them believe this is a free choice. It must be emphasized that compulsory heterosexuality need not rely on extreme bigotry against homosexuality in order to achieve its goal of instituting the heterosexual couple as the *sine qua non* of personal success and social stability.

Heterosexism is not only present when someone actively discriminates against or harasses a gay person. It is also present in many places where gay people are not involved, for example in bridal industry ads that portray diamonds and white wedding dresses, and indirectly traditional marriage, as universally desirable. In this sense, heterosexism oppresses not only homosexuals but anyone who is either celibate or is in a casual sexual relationship. It is even oppressive to coupled heterosexuals who enjoy its privileges, since the whole weight of a social institution is imposed upon their individual shoulders. Bridal industry ads are offensive to married women who are happy in their marriage but do not derive their identity from it. Women who want to take a job in a different city and feel guilty about commuting between job and husband are also oppressed by heterosexism. The relationship is supposed to be more important to them than to the husband, who would not be expected to have to make those choices.

Although heterosexism oppresses gay men and all men who do not fit "the norm," it weighs particularly heavily on women. Women suffer more pressure to "find a man" than men do to find a wife. Women are the ones who are constantly being told—by the advertising industry, movies and novels, and by family and friends—that they have to work at improving their appearance and their cuisine in order to get a man, or if they have one, to keep him. Men gain extra social status from having a woman at their beck and call, and can be stigmatized as "queers" if they fail to produce a woman for the appropriate social occasions. However men do not need female validation for their very identity. They change neither their name nor their social class upon marriage. A garbageman married to a schoolteacher is still a garbageman; a university-educated woman who marries a farmer becomes "the farmer's wife." We see then that because women are denied an autonomous identity, the consequences of being in or out of a heterosexual couple are greater for them.

The success of the single working woman is seen, and often experienced by the woman herself, as clouded or even negated by her single status. The executive woman who is not with a man is assumed to have sacrificed her womanhood for her career, and this sacrifice is usually regarded as the wrong choice.

Heterosexism is also at work in the social perception of women's poverty. Poor women who are single or widowed are treated as special cases, whose poverty is attributed to the lack of a male provider. In reality, their poverty is not caused by the absence of the increasingly mythical male provider, but by such factors as the wage gap between men and women, women's responsibility for children after divorce, and the refusal of governments to grant pensions to homemakers. These sexist and heterosexist social and economic policies are rarely perceived as the cause of women's poverty.

Compulsory heterosexuality perpetuates the wage gap and job ghettoization by telling women that they are at some point going to be taken care of by men. Furthermore it reinforces social and economic inequality by eroticizing the power imbalances that exist between men and women. As sociologist Margaret Ann Jensen points out in *Love's Sweet Return: The Harlequin Story*, this is a common element in mass-market women's romances. Jensen describes the attractiveness of what would otherwise be known as "sexual harassment":

> Increasingly, when heroines are working for heroes, as is frequently the case, they are subjected to sexual harassment. Of course, it is not interpreted as such within the stories because the heroine is in love with the hero and ultimately marries him, but it is sexual harassment . . . The element of unwillingness or coercion adds to the excitement and tension of the romance.[9]

Because the reader of Harlequins is expected to adhere to the dictates of compulsory heterosexuality, she is expected to interpret sexual coercion by a man in a superior position as permissible. After all, clerks and secretaries lead boring lives and are, according to the ideology, always sighing for a man to sweep them off their feet and away from the typewriter. The reader also knows from reading other Harlequins that the hero will in the end marry his subordinate, and so he is exonerated from any accusation of exploitation. Marriage, as permanent heterosexuality, justifies all means used to achieve it. After all, if heroines were to rebuff all advances by males in positions of authority, they would never get married, would they? Or at least, they would never, by marrying, acquire a new social identity.

Women know heterosexual reality is not like either fairy tales or Harlequins. However most women learned this only after some years of experience. Because we are surrounded by heterosexist ideology we enter heterosexual relationships accompanied by a whole series of expectations and ideals about what "it" is supposed to be like. Whether our fantasy entails being swept off our feet by a tall millionaire, or whether we sigh after a non-sexist man in a crumpled shirt, we all have expectations and hopes and we are all more or less affected by the stories of "great loves" we have read about or seen in movies. From Romeo and Juliet to the soaps there is a constant stream of ideology about what heterosexuality is like or should be like.

By contrast, the almost complete dearth of images of lesbianism in our culture means that when a woman begins to feel attracted to other women she has no preconceived notion of what "it" is supposed to look or feel like. The few lesbian enclaves in large cities have created some ideal conceptions of what love between women is or could be about. But these ideals are not part of the general culture, and to seek them out one has to visit feminist or gay bookstores, listen to hard-to-get lesbian songs, or attend the few and not widely publicized events the community organizes. Even for those lesbians living in large cities where lesbian communities do exist, one has to make a real effort to go out and find the like-minded women and the culture that speaks to us. The culture of heterosexism, of course, washes over us constantly.

When I began to fall in love with a woman, I was completely unacquainted with *any* depictions of lesbianism. The descriptions and ideals produced by lesbian feminism had never come to my attention, and I did not become aware of them until I was already deep into the most intense love relationship of my life. I thus did not expect or hope or fantasize: I simply explored with great wonder everything that happened in those early months of our love, all the feelings and thoughts that seemed to be arising out of the blue in my previously "normal" heart.

Years earlier prior to my heterosexual awakening I had moped around for years fantasizing about fulfilment through a relationship with a man. I cannot emphasize strongly enough what a difference it makes to one's sexual experience when you have to simply accept the present and invent the future. Everything—from how to physically make love, to how to describe my new relationship to my family—had to be invented. A lesbian relationship has to be creative, whether the women in it are inherently creative or not. The lesbian feminist poet Adrienne Rich has put this very well:

> The rules break like a thermometer,
> quicksilver spills across the charted systems,
> we're out in a country that has no language
> no laws, we're chasing the raven and the wren
> through gorges unexplored since dawn
> whatever we do together is pure invention
> the maps they gave us were out of date
> by years . . .
>   (Poem XIII, Twenty-One Love Poems)[10]

Such unexplored, uncharted terrain necessitates the creativity which characterizes lesbian relationships. We don't even have many stereotypes to resist, unlike gay men whose adolescence and coming-out process are marked by the image of The Faggot, with his mannerisms, his unmanly occupations, his lisp, his love of clothes. All we have by way of negative stereotypes are a few broken snatches, a half-remembered article about Gertrude Stein, a vision of a cigar-smoking tough woman with her hands in her jean pockets. These are not powerful myths; they're fragments of social maps we instantly know to be "out of date by years." The lesbian may make a cameo appearance as a wicked sex fiend or a butch truck driver, but paradoxically 99 percent of the time the lesbian is merely invisible.

THE INVISIBILITY OF LESBIAN EROTIC POWER

When I was about seven or eight years old, I became aware of something odd in my extended family. There were two older women known by us and by all my family's friends as "the aunts." They were somehow related to my cousins, at whose home we spent a lot of time, especially during summer holidays. One day I asked my mother what their connection was, since it seemed clear they weren't really my cousins' aunts. My mother said something about one of them being related to my cousins' live-in grandmother, and she described her inseparable companion as being more than a good friend. I don't remember my mother's exact words, but I was left with the impression that the two "aunts" had lived together since they were young and loved each other like sisters, or even more. I was satisfied with that answer; but something struck me as in need of explanation when, playing hide-and-seek in my cousins' house, I went into their room to hide and saw they had two twin beds pushed together, just as my parents did. My cousins were wealthy and had a big house with a room for each of their two maids, so it was odd that the aunts would be living in closer quarters than my sister and me in our smaller home. But I couldn't put my finger on it. Now, the interesting thing is that the two aunts were universally accepted as part of the extended family, even though one of them smoked cigars, swore like a trooper, and wore the shortest hair I'd ever seen on a middle-aged woman, while the other had silver curls and behaved like a proper lady. The lady-like one was always saying to the other, "For heaven's sake, don't drive so fast" and other wife-like things. All the while her butch partner, in a loud bass voice, continued to swear at drivers who competed with her for possession of the road. Their couple behaviour was the object of much teasing, but our cousins loved them. I was tremendously pleased when I once went with my cousins to spend the Holy Week holiday in the aunts' Madrid apartment. The large apartment was full of red velvet curtains and large oil paintings. Their moderate wealth came from a jointly owned pin factory which we kids visited with much curiosity.

The two aunts were as obvious a lesbian couple as ever graced the halls of the Spanish bourgeoisie. And yet they were neither ostracized nor ridiculed, and were trusted with children as one would trust any female relative. But their respectability was obtained at the price of remaining silent about their love and about their lesbianism. Not wanting to live in isolation, they had to collude with their relatives in pretending that they were just "the aunts," elderly spinsters living on the edges of "real" families.

I cannot imagine two gay men being able to maintain family relations as the aunts did. If an obviously gay man had lived in our family, his lover would certainly not have acquired uncle status and neither man would have been trusted with children or consistently included in gatherings. This is undoubtedly because even a child could have spotted a faggot, while the lesbian aunts were not seen as a threat to proper gender formation in the younger generation. They were just a harmless, picturesque pair of aunts in a large and raucous family with an abundance of eccentric female relatives. They were not taken very seriously.

Invisibility does have some advantages. Many lesbians even today can "pass" as heterosexual women even as they carry on love relationships under the noses of relatives and coworkers. Two women can put their arms around each other in public and, as long as they take care not to kiss or look into each other's eyes too long, they will probably be left alone. This is changing, however, especially in cities like Toronto. Two women holding hands are now usually regarded with homophobic suspicion, whereas ten years ago a more innocent interpretation would have prevailed. Nevertheless, despite the higher profile of lesbianism female roommates are not immediately assumed to be lovers. And since strict butch/femme roles are almost extinct, people who cling to the old stereotypes will not recognize two ordinary-looking women walking down the street in mutual delight as "Lesbians."

But invisibility is not really a blessing. Invisibility means society refuses to admit the existence of love between women. Or, if its existence is acknowledged, the love in question is not regarded as real love or real sex, much less as really womanly. Most people are unable to imagine sex between women. They ask "But what do lesbians do in bed anyway?" as though in the absence of the phallic King the serfs were unable to do anything worthy of the name of sex.

Let us examine some of the prevalent myths and fantasies about lesbian sexuality. One common fantasy sees lesbianism as immature but basically harmless. It imagines two women fleeing from the slings and arrows of heterosexuality, cuddling in each other's arms and lightly kissing each other's cheeks before falling asleep like children. The assumption behind this myth (one to which unfortunately many heterosexual feminists subscribe) is that "real women" have sex with men. The fantasy which probably characterizes male thoughts on the lesbian question is the one which sees lesbians as super-whores, sex fiends who need to molest, humiliate or even torture a defenceless sexual object, namely another woman. The sexual object is invariably imagined as "not a real lesbian." This fantasy characterizes the "lesbian porn" found in *Penthouse* and elsewhere. A subtler version is found in such serious works as biographies of famous literary lesbians. Quentin Bell's renowned biography of Virginia Woolf portrays Woolf as an essentially sexless woman who was the object of the passions of several powerful lesbians (including Vita Sackville-West). Victoria Glendinning's biography of Vita, while not overtly judgemental, quotes from letters between Vita and her women lovers in order to imply that Vita's lesbianism involved sexual cruelty. The "evidence" for this is an unimportant allusion by one lover to a small bruise acquired during lovemaking.[11] Glendinning's biography does not question Vita's tendency to escape from difficult lesbian love affairs by pleading the importance of her marriage to Harold Nicolson (who, like Vita, was primarily homosexual). It never occurs to Glendinning that perhaps it was socially convenient for both Harold and Vita to pretend to the world, and to each other as well, that their homosexual relationships were shot through with the lower passions while their marriage was the true work of intelligent minds.

The fact is that lesbian sexual relationships do not follow any one model. Like heterosexual relationships, they can be purely sexual or primarily emotional and intellectual. Sometimes lesbians only want to cuddle and kiss, but that is not evidence of sexual immaturity. At other times the same women might feel rather raunchy, and spend several hours in passionate, strong sex. Sometimes we want to be comforted and held, while at other times we want to use our physical strength and feel the full force of our lover's passion.

This is not to say that lesbians never fall into ruts, or that there are not lesbians who are as narrow in their sexual tastes as teenagers who only like McDonald's hamburgers. Boredom in the bedroom is not monopolized by married couples. However, there is one initial advantage to lesbian sex: there are no conveniently traditional roles to fall back upon. There is no missionary position.

Apart from being potentially versatile, lesbian sex can be tremendously powerful. It is of course true that any strong love, or any strong sexual urge, unleashes a powerful force in human beings. But without entering into competition for the Olympic sex medal, one can claim that the unique power of lesbian eroticism is one of the strongest forces in human existence. It is not a matter of innate gender differences; rather we are socially conditioned to *expect* other women to nurture us. Generally speaking, women *are* more "emotional" than men, or at least are trained to express their emotions more than men. This means that in heterosexual relationships the emotional depth is often limited by men's tendency to steer clear of "heavy" emotions, and by women's knowledge that men will seldom be able to take good care of an emotionally vulnerable partner. Yet with another woman it is easier to let go, to be vulnerable, to abolish the boundaries that usually keep egos apart and distinct.

Unfortunately, this facility for bonding with another woman is not an unmixed blessing. Many lesbians become vulnerable to a lover too soon, and expect her to lower her own defenses immediately. They fall in love too quickly and too deeply, setting themselves up for tragic disappointments. Because of this "emotionalism" that women are conditioned to have, and the inevitable associations of the lover's body with the nurturing, all-powerful body of the mother, love between women can create some of the strongest bonds in human experience. But it is equally true that the breaking of these bonds, or even the distant threat of a break, can wreak untold havoc on women's psyches and bring about a case of separation anxiety.

The love one woman has for another can be protective and generous; but it can also be violently selfish and jealous. Often these contradictory qualities are found in one and the same person, who alternates between a deep, giving love and a raging jealousy bordering on hatred. This may be one reason why intense and emotionally fraught love triangles are, though not common, a feature of lesbian life. The emotional thermometer fluctuates wildly but the triangle persists partly because of the strange bond that is created between the "rivals" who have the potential to love and nurture one another as well as to evoke the worst fears of maternal deprivation.[12]

The erotic power of lesbianism then, based as it is on certain specifically feminine characteristics, is as much a mixed blessing as feminine emotionalism itself. Exhausted by overly emotional relationships, many a lesbian has been known to long for the more detached sexual relationships that characterize gay male life. And yet the intensity of lesbian erotic attachment is also a strength and a source of joy.

When the tendency to instantly turn up the volume on any and all sexual relationships is checked by a realistic assessment of the situation, then fleeting attractions can be valued for no more than what they are. The extreme *égoisme à deux* of lesbian "fusion" relationships can be quite damaging, especially when one partner suddenly feels her autonomy slipping and decides to reassert her independence. And it is damaging even when both partners collude to create a tight relationship in which each is half a couple instead of a whole person. However, one learns through experience, and it is possible to retain some of the generosity, passion and mutual vulnerability of the woman-to-woman connection while tempering it by a lasting commitment to friends, work, community and children.

LESBIANS, THE STATE, AND SOCIETY

Most people think we live in enlightened times, and that out-right persecution of lesbians and other unpopular minorities is confined to outposts of bigotry. Most people are unaware that divorced women are routinely deprived of custody of their children if ex-husbands bring evidence of lesbianism into the courtroom. Few people know that as late as the seventies there were cases in Canada of women being committed to psychiatric hospitals and subjected to heavy drugs and electroshock because their parents or husbands convinced doctors that lesbianism was a sign of madness. And today, many young lesbians are forced out of their homes by irate fathers.

It is important to understand that lesbians are not only subjected to occasional persecutions but also to the everyday grind of societal oppression. Constant tension and stress is felt even by those lesbians living in relatively privileged settings. Every day we have to decide how we will appear before the world. Should I, in a coffee-break conversation with cowork-ers, speak about "my lover" the way other women talk about their boyfriends? Will I hide all the tell-tale lesbian books and posters in my home because an aunt is visiting? Should I write a letter to the newspaper protesting an article that called femin-ists "hairy-legged dykes," suffering the stress of seeing my name publicly associated with lesbianism? Or should I just suffer the aggravation in silence? For lesbians, the most trivial daily occurrence can give rise to the ever-present dilemma of silent anger versus public confrontation, self-denial versus risk.

However lesbians choose to respond to specific situations— and there is not a lesbian alive who can possibly be "out of the closet" in all circumstances—they are not free to simply live their lives without making an "issue" of their lesbianism. If they try to avoid the stress of going public they will succeed only in internalizing the conflict, and making themselves un-happy by the constant self-censorship which alone can keep the closet door shut. On the other hand, if one tells one's fam-ily and friends about one's sexual choices, one is not then exempt from future dilemmas. Many lesbians struggle for years with the difficult question of telling one's parents, only to discover that after the "big talk" silence once more descends upon them. A common pattern goes as follows: 1) a lesbian will steel herself and "come out" to a friend or relative; 2) there will be a "big talk" in which the friend or relative either freaks out or pretends it does not matter in the least; 3) there will be a period in which the friend or relative ponders the information, while the lesbian worries about what people will think of her; 4) the friend or relative will act as though once the subject has been disposed of it never need be referred to again. Short of pointedly bringing a lover everywhere she goes or rudely interrupting conversations with "lesbian comments," the lesbian will find that it is very difficult to integrate her lesbian life into her work or family life, or even into her friendship networks. This is the main reason why lesbians tend to form friendships with other lesbians, and maintain only a few heterosexual friends who are often kept separate from the rest of her life.

Social prejudice and heterosexist attitudes are certainly one big obstacle preventing lesbians from living freely. However, the mechanisms of the state (laws, courts, police, school systems) are not at all neutral with respect to lesbians. For instance, in Canada it is illegal to engage in gay sex until one is twenty-one years old, while the heterosexual age of consent is fourteen or sixteen depending on the province. It is of course not likely that two twenty-year-old university students would be prosecuted for sleeping together. But if an eighteen-year-old woman sleeps with her thirty-year-old teacher, the older woman might well be subject to criminal sanctions (especially if the younger woman's parents find out).

A case in point. In 1981 there was an incident outside a Toronto lesbian bar in which two plainclothes policemen roughed up some young women. At the press conference held to denounce this police brutality, the media were completely uninterested in reporting on the police misconduct. Instead, they turned the tables on the victims and asked if the women in question had been dressed "as women or as men"! The implication appeared to be that if they had been dressed as men, then they were asking for it, just like rape victims who happened to be wearing what society may think of as "sexy" clothes.

Another case in point. It is the policy of the U.S. department of immigration not to allow "avowed" homosexuals into the country. Because of this, Canadian lesbians who travel to the annual Michigan Women's Music Festival are routinely subjected to humiliating interrogations at border checkpoints. One woman I know was repeatedly asked by a male immigration officer when the last time was that she had been fucked by a man.

The police and the bureaucracy are not the only agencies of the state that exercise their power in such a way as to reinforce lesbian oppression. Lesbians are also often deprived of custody of their children by the courts. Furthermore, lesbian couples are not allowed to adopt children under the rules of Children's Aid, and a lesbian who wants to be artificially inseminated will find it virtually impossible to find a sympathetic doctor who will help her. Fortunately new networks have developed to allow lesbians who want to have children to get in touch with volunteer gay men, but these networks are almost underground.

Because of all these problems, legal change is one of the demands of the lesbian/gay movement. For instance, if sexual orientation were included in the Canadian Charter of Rights and in provincial human rights codes as one of the prohibited grounds of discrimination, gay people would have a basis from which to fight the discriminatory employment regulations now in effect in government, the army, and on school boards. Such legal changes would not in themselves change much—Quebec's human rights code does include sexual orientation but gay men still get arrested in bars and baths—but they could provide a partial basis from which to challenge heterosexism.

But legal changes must go hand in hand with changes in the public perception of homosexuality. Just as one of the first tasks of the post-1968 women's movement was to challenge the media stereotypes of women and to project new, positive images of women's strength and capabilities, so one of the key tasks of lesbian communities is to present an alternative image of who we are.

Newspapers, radio and television seldom have anything to say about lesbians, good or bad. We can conclude that their main function is to make lesbianism invisible and continue the pretence that every woman is or would like to be attached to a man. But the one branch of the mass media that does concern itself with lesbianism is the mass-market porn publication. Because these products are explicitly aimed at men, few heterosexual women and even fewer lesbians are aware of what images of lesbians are found in these glossy publications whose sales are in the millions. *Penthouse* sells five million copies every month. One-tenth of these sales are in Canada. In a six month period in 1980, *Penthouse* grossed close to eight million dollars in Canada alone, *Playboy* almost four million dollars.

Pornography does not present a unified image of lesbians or of sex between women. Lesbians have been portrayed as sex-craved, aggressive and sadistic females who revel in the lascivious pursuit of sweet female flesh. When they get their just desserts by either committing suicide or, as in the film version of D.H. Lawrence's "The Fox," being killed by falling trees, the public is expected to be relieved that the sweet young female in question can now become the property of a man. Lesbians have also been portrayed as pseudo men wearing ties and bowler hats and swaggering around bars smoking cigars. This stereotype of the butch can intersect with that of the "evil female," but it remains a distinct image, emphasizing mannish appearance rather than sex.

There is another stereotype which, while present in male literature and pornography for hundreds of years, has seen a recent dramatic rise in popularity. It involves depicting sex between women as relatively harmless because it is shown as disconnected from a social lesbian identity and from feminist politics. This stereotype presents lesbian sex as a kinky diversion, the ultimate in swinging. The women involved are neither mannish nor evil, and perhaps because of that are not engaged in serious competition with men for access to sweet female flesh. I would like to focus on this particular stereotype, for it is much more common in soft-core porn than the now old-fashioned stereotype of the evil hag. The old stereotypes do not hold much sway among women, especially if they have a sense of feminism, and they certainly do not shape lesbians' self-image. But the new trivialized representation of lesbianism as a relatively harmless erotic exoticism has the potential to affect even people who would not be swayed by obviously misogynist stereotypes. And in a subtle way it could even affect the development of today's lesbian communities.

Penthouse, which prides itself on sexual libertarianism and opposition to the American Moral Majority, has pioneered this new image of lesbian sex as non-threatening to both male pleasure and male authority. This has been done primarily in the columns devoted to readers' letters and queries, the *Penthouse* "Forum" and Xaviera Hollander's regular column. Whether or not the letters are actually written by readers, and whether they are descriptions of real experiences or only fantasies, is irrelevant. The point is that the texts are read as if they realistically portrayed spontaneous sexual experience, and hence function as models of how to interpret the reader's erotic life.

In one randomly chosen issue of *Penthouse* (August 1982), letters to the "Forum" contain the whole spectrum of *Penthouse*'s representation of lesbianism. The first story/fantasy involving lesbians is told from the point of view of a young man who describes himself as "your average American teenager." He writes that he and his friend Sam saw "four beautiful chicks" in a bar who appeared to be making out with each other. The boys got instantly horny, and "we got up the balls to go over by the table and ask them if we could buy them a drink." The women said yes. The level of horniness keeps going up, until the "leader" of the women's gang (who has short hair dyed green!) invites the two men over to "our place." The partying starts anew and two women begin making love with each other, while the other two have a go at the boys, without however bringing them to orgasm. The women, having teased the men, now reveal the existence of an s/m dungeon full of "leather, chains, whips, dildos, vibrators—everything you could imagine a girl using." The women, we are told, "turned into animals," threatening the men and directing them to perform various sexual acts. Interestingly enough, they do not suggest the men make it with each other. Anyway, the men begin to lose their fear and to enjoy the sex; their panic about sadistic dykes turns into lust and the evening ends in an orgy.

Although there are hints of the "lesbian-as-witch" stereotype, the overall effect of the letter is not to make lesbians appear horrible and demonic but only bizarre. Their "bossiness" toward men is as much an indication of harmless peculiarity as their use of sex toys or green hair dye. Yet, if this is the explicit message of the text, there is an implicit message which contradicts it and taps into the age-old "male dread of women." The women are presented as both rejecting men and lusting after them. They are sexually frustrated bitches who will not admit their longing for the phallus. The fun-loving punkers are distant relatives of the medieval witch.

The second story is free from sado-masochistic imagery and more ambiguous in its portrayal of lesbians' attitudes toward men. It is entitled "The Barter System," and is told from the point of view of two college boys who decide to scalp tickets for a Rolling Stones concert. Two college "girls" "who were rumoured to be lesbians" approach them for tickets. (The young women are described as "foxy"; clearly, men have caught on to the fact that many lesbians look like ordinary girls.) The two girls tell the guys they are gay, and the guys pretend to be surprised. The guys are genuinely surprised, however, when the women suggest a barter: if the boys take a few dollars off the (inflated) price of the tickets, then they'll "perform" for the men. The boys lower their price from fifty dollars to thirty and settle down to watch the two women make love. Predictably, they soon join in the fun. Indeed, the boys have so much fun that they generously lower the price of their tickets to twenty dollars. Everyone is pleased with the barter, and the boys conclude it was "hard to believe that the two were gay, since they had given us such a good time."

The moral of the story is to not believe the stereotypical view that all lesbians are ugly and hate men. And, even if it is rumoured that certain foxy women are lesbians, they are still legitimate objects of male desire. Every lesbian has her price, we are told. Thus, "fun with lesbians" is constructed as a new pastime for imaginative males, one which adds an exotic variation to their repertoire while reassuring them that no aspect of female sexuality is really beyond the male gaze and grasp.

The apparently open-minded attitude toward lesbians illustrated here is not an indication of the acceptance of true sexual variety, for this open-mindedness is not extended to men who turn their backs on heterosexuality. *Penthouse* pretends to like lesbians but is full of homophobic comments against gay men. And if faggots who refuse to fuck women are not welcome because male readers do not want to suffer the anxiety of feeling aroused by a homosexual story, neither are dykes who resolutely refuse to be fucked by men and who opt out of "The Barter System."

There are some letters in the "Forum" however that seem to eliminate the male presence in their depiction of lesbianism. These are few and far between, but they are important to analyze, for any examples of lesbian autonomy presented in a positive light would certainly indicate that there are more chinks in the pornographer's armour than feminists have thought. So let us now turn to the one letter which appealed most strongly to me as a lesbian. This was written, we are told, by a thirty-five-year-old divorced woman who comes home one evening to find her daughter fondling and kissing her two girlfriends. The woman is surprised to find out that she is turned on by this scene, which she witnesses without being seen, a privilege usually granted only to men. After some developments in the plot, the woman ends up making love with one of her daughter's girlfriends who, although presented initially as inexperienced, suddenly produces a double-headed dildo. Dildoes, incidentally, are virtually unknown among lesbians, though vibrators are certainly becoming popular. But *Penthouse* house style requires that lesbians be depicted with penis-substitutes, presumably so that the male reader can imagine himself replacing the dildo by the "real" thing. So there is still a place, even in the seemingly all-female world of lesbian sex, for the male phallus to shine—as a piece of plastic if not in the flesh. And to drive the point home, the divorced woman reassures the male reader that despite having discovered the delights of lesbianism, "I still love men."

Thus we see that even those depictions of lesbianism which do not show men actually fucking the alleged lesbians make ample room for the symbolic phallus, and explicitly refrain from challenging male assumptions about having access to all women. If a lesbian reader was turned on by some of the less sexist fantasies she read in *Penthouse* and decided to send in her own story, she would find that her experiences would be censored. If she finished the letter by saying: " . . . and after the wonderful experience with Susie, I never wanted to look at a man again, and I lived happily ever after in the lesbian community," her letter would not see the light of day.

Lesbianism is thus robbed of its radical potential because it is portrayed as compatible with heterosexuality, or rather as part of heterosexuality itself. The contradictions that our society creates between hetero- and homosexuality are wished away and social oppression is ignored. Because lesbians have become more socially visible, *Penthouse* has taken it upon itself to reassure men that these lesbians are not a real threat. They ultimately need the phallus, even if they resent this need or do not admit to it. The prospect of a non-trivial lesbianism that unfolds all the erotic and political power inherent in relationships between women is not a prospect that pornography can afford to contemplate. It must therefore dispel the "rumours" that some "foxy college girls" are no longer interested in men.

Sex between women then is not necessarily a threat; it can be incorporated into the phallic pornographic universe. What is threatening, and what most men are unable to imagine, is a fulfilled female life that proceeds independently of men.

This life is precisely what has to be imagined if lesbianism is going to become a valid social choice, a way of life that is open to any woman and not just to a heroic few who dare to leave behind family, friends, and respectability. It is autonomy and self-determination, not kinky sex, which characterizes our growing lesbian culture. And it will be this culture that produces the images to counteract the false images of porn.[13]

LESBIAN CULTURE

If by lesbian culture we mean not just erotic representations of sex between women, but a celebration of the many aspects of lesbian life including eroticism, then it is clear that lesbian culture is rooted in feminist traditions that have presented positive images of women's power and autonomy. Heterosexual feminists since Mary Wollstonecraft have tried to show how traditional feminine dependence distorts women's growth. There is a continuum of feminist thought which links those early calls for autonomy with today's cultural production of lesbians like Adrienne Rich, Holly Near, Jane Rule, Marie-Claire Blais, Jovette Marchessault and many other lesser known women of varying ethnic backgrounds, classes, and nationalities.

This is not to say there is no break between heterosexual feminist and lesbian culture. For instance, many of Holly Near's songs appeal to all women and present love relationships without specifying "he" or "she." But some of her songs have a special significance for lesbians, such as "Imagine My Surprise," which deals with her own coming out as a lesbian.

There are a couple of themes that emerge from an examination of the lesbian culture that has developed over the past ten or fifteen years. I am talking primarily about lesbian literature, and to a lesser extent music, since we have not yet been able to make many films or produce much visual art. This is partly due to financial factors and sale and distribution problems. But it is also due to certain inherent problems in portraying women's bodies erotically without having those depictions interpreted as pornographic. In any case, in women's, gay, and progressive bookstores one can find quite a number of literary works that allow us to make some tentative comments about trends and recurring ideals.

The first thing that strikes the reader of lesbian fiction is that a lot of it is hopelessly romantic. In an age where heterosexual women write about relationships primarily in the tragic mode, lesbians often write to celebrate perfect and enduring love. Many of the paperback novels known as "lesbian trash" follow the traditional romance formula in presenting a lonely lesbian who eventually finds self-discovery and love. And biographies of famous lesbians often suffer from the same tendency to romanticize love between women. More recently, it has become somewhat passé to celebrate the isolated couple. *The Ladies of Langollen* and *Patience and Sarah* were popular books ten years ago, but now they are not. A common theme in today's lesbian books is the romanticization not of the couple but of the community. A good example is Marie-Claire Blais's beautifully written novel *Les Nuits de l'Underground* (*Nights in the Underground*). In this novel set in contemporary

Montreal, lesbians, whether single or in couples, are presented warts and all. But the community emerges as the collective heroine freeing itself from the long Montreal winter and the dark bar in order to begin a community project in the new light of spring.

The relative dearth of truly superior lesbian works of literature is not a historical accident. Early lesbian writers (that is, anyone writing more than ten years ago) did not start with a clean slate. They had to confront various stereotypes and prejudices in their work, and overcompensate for them by creating heroines free from all moral taint. One could not have written about a lesbian who happened to be a kleptomaniac without book reviewers leaping to the conclusion that all lesbians live by shoplifting.

Because of this need to redeem lesbianism from society's moral stigma, it was rather difficult to realistically portray lust and sex between women. Apart from the problems inhibiting all female writers from dealing frankly with the pleasures of the body, lesbian writers laboured under additional prohibitions and dilemmas. What if they described a lurid bedroom scene and men started to buy the book as pornography? What if the book was deemed unpublishable simply because it dealt with lesbianism? What if other lesbians criticized the author for concentrating on the erotic and thus giving credence to the myth that lesbians are essentially defined by their lust?

It has only been very recently, in the wake of a general turn toward erotically explicit but non-pornographic writing by women, that it has been possible to begin describing sex between women from a lesbian perspective. But even now the whole question of erotic writing is an extremely difficult one, and only the best of writers can manage to get around the difficulties that stand in the way of this important task.

It will be possible for lesbians to write "great works" featuring lesbians only when lesbianism is less of an issue, less of an "exceptional" state. Today, any depiction of lesbianism risks being seen as a depiction of all lesbians. After seeing the 1982 movie *Personal Best* (directed by Robert Towne) many people began to suspect all female athletes of being lesbians and, conversely, all lesbians of being jocks. Lesbian writers also suffer from the weight of the long-suppressed expectations of a community in search of positive images. It is difficult to depict a lesbian as an ordinary human being with flaws and contradictions when we know that her every fault will be attributed to her lesbianism.

A more recent film directed by Doris Deitch (1986) shows a very different, more lesbian-positive possibility. *Desert Hearts* is based on Jane Rule's ground-breaking lesbian romance of the early sixties, *Desert of the Heart*. The movie's main character is a female academic who goes off to Reno, Nevada, to obtain a divorce. In the six weeks that it takes to get her papers she gets more an education in love and lust than she had ever acquired in her years of teaching literature at Columbia. Her educator is a beautiful young woman who works in a casino and is the town's notorious but not unloved lesbian. The movie verges on schmaltz, but in any case one does not go to see this movie for high intellectual content. Rather one goes for the sheer pleasure of watching the two gorgeous women flirt at great lengths, fall in love, and perform a very passionate love scene for our unabashed voyeuristic pleasure.

I discussed the film with a lesbian-feminist artist, and it occurred to us that watching *Desert Hearts* gave us the undiluted, uncomplicated pleasure that men probably get from watching mainstream movies. The film is designed by and for women who enjoy women's bodies. We are able to experience sexual pleasure in a context in which we know beforehand (most Canadian lesbians have read the book) that the women will indeed fall in love and have sex. We never have to worry about male violence or about the possibility of tragedy. Furthermore, the mountain scenery, the admittedly mainstream beauty of the women, the pleasant lighting and music, the costumes and the movie as a whole provide a most agreeable environment both for the characters and for our own pleasure. Since female desire, including lesbian desire, is so seldom fulfilled in mainstream, male-oriented movies, *Desert Hearts* is a rare treat. The camera eye does not have to be the male gaze in technological disguise.

THE WOMEN'S MOVEMENT:
LESBIANISM IS AN ISSUE FOR ALL FEMINISTS

If we look at lesbianism as a social category identifying women who are permanently independent from men and look to each other for love, sex, and day-to-day support, then it is clearly in the interest of all feminists to defend lesbianism as a positive choice. Conversely, when lesbians are sneered at for being "too ugly to get a man" or for "aping men," heterosexual feminism is also being attacked. All women are kept down and prevented from freely choosing if and how they will relate to men or conform to male standards of feminity. Thus, defending lesbian rights and supporting lesbian culture is not something that heterosexual feminists ought to do as a matter of charity; rather defending lesbianism is an integral part of the struggle for women's independence. Attacks on lesbians are implicitly attacks on all women who deviate from the traditional pattern. If heterosexual feminists expect to increase the social space for women, they have to defend the right of all women to choose lesbianism if they so desire.

Unfortunately, not all feminists see the issue this way, because not all have grappled with internalized homophobia and heterosexism. Many heterosexual feminists are uneasy about lesbians speaking publicly for the women's movement, because they fear people will get "the wrong impression" and dismiss all feminists as man-hating lesbians. Instead of challenging this prejudice, many heterosexual feminists run away from it and give in to it. In the early seventies, the American National Organization for Women (NOW) carried out a witch-hunt against lesbians precisely because it did not want to "create the wrong impression" and ruin its public image. The irony of this purge was that the divisions and hard feelings it caused were probably far worse for the organization's morale and cohesion than anything male attacks on lesbian feminism might have caused. Today, mainstream women's organizations would probably not undertake the same kind of divisive marginalization of lesbians. But nevertheless, lesbians are often perceived within the mainstream women's movements as "uncomfortably sexual," as Lorna Weir has put it.[14]

Heterosexual feminists tend to have a certain split between their private erotic life with men and their political activities with women. But for lesbian feminists "the personal is political" in a much more direct way. Often, political coworkers are also lovers (or ex-lovers, or the ex-lovers of one's present lover!). There is an unmistakable erotic energy that sometimes surfaces not just in social gatherings but even in meetings or more formal settings. Grassroots feminist organizations often accept this, but more "respectable" organizations frown on any manifestations of lesbian erotic energy or even on women who talk about lesbian sexuality. The annual meetings of Canada's national feminist coalition, the National Action Committee for the Status of Women (NAC), rarely break the silence about lesbianism although, encouragingly, the 1985 annual general meeting included a lesbian caucus and a strong pro-lesbian rights resolution.

Lesbians are, in this day and age, seldom persecuted within feminist organizations. But as a rule they are expected to keep quiet about their specific concerns and to speak in public always from the point of view of a mythical "average woman" who is assumed to be heterosexual and white. Lesbians who break this rule are perceived as particularistic, divisive, and even frivolous. And they themselves internalize this view and suppress their specific concerns. During a public forum on pornography held in Toronto as part of the 1984 International Women's Day celebration, I was in the uncomfortable position of having to represent the "lesbian viewpoint," speaking after a noted mainstream feminist (married and with children) represented the "average" woman's point of view. When I suggested that the interests of lesbians in matters of erotic representation and obscenity legislation might not be well served by censorship provisions, given the likelihood that our own culture would be censored by the state, the mainstream feminist looked at me as though I had just broken some sacred feminist tablet and had sprouted horns and a tail. And I myself felt awkward, as though I was the one who was being "divisive." But the fact of the matter is that the other woman was not being inclusive by failing to recognize the specific concerns of lesbians. The politics of the women's movement are often set by articulate, well-educated women who are usually middle-class, white, and heterosexual (publicly at least). Their point of view is presented as being that of women in general. By contrast, lesbians, women of colour and other "minority" women are seen as representing only women like themselves and not women in general. Lesbian issues are constructed as "particularistic," "special-interest" issues. Women who are known to be lesbians are treated, by the media and even by many feminists, as unable to speak about anything *but* lesbian issues, as though lesbians did not need equal pay and indeed pensions as much as anyone else. This is heterosexism at work. To be heterosexual is regarded as average, normal, and non-problematic. But to be anything else is instantly problematic and relegates one to the status of "minority." And if no vocal members of that minority group are present to voice their views, then their concerns will be routinely forgotten. A feminist movement that claims to speak for all women must make sure that it does in fact include the concerns and views of all sectors, without falling into the trap of dividing women into "normal" or "average" on the one hand, and "fringe" groups on the other.

Seen from this perspective, it becomes clear that lesbianism is an issue for *all* feminists, just as child care and child rearing is an issue for all feminists regardless of whether or not they are mothers. For example, almost all feminist organizations have a clear position on women's right to abortion, and many lesbians have worked long and hard to defend this right even though they do not personally need abortion facilities. This is because it has become clear that what is at stake is not just abortion itself, but the larger right of all women to make their choices around childbearing and sexuality free from state and church coercion. Similarly then, when lesbians fight to gain access to the media or other public spaces, what is really at stake is the right of *all* women to define their own sexual identity and have access to cultural resources in order to create positive images of their eroticism and their lifestyle. All women who long for a woman-centred sexuality will find it in their best interests to take an active interest in the development of lesbian culture. To fight for lesbian rights and against heterosexism is to fight against male-defined feminine roles, and for autonomy. Active support for lesbian cultural and political initiatives is hence an integral part of being a feminist.

When heterosexual feminists fail to support lesbian initiatives, it is not only through incorrect political ideas. It is also because certain emotional reactions and gut feelings prevent them from thinking clearly. Lesbians by their very presence often make heterosexual women uncomfortable and anxious. These anxieties have to be examined one by one and dealt with in a calm manner, always remembering they are not individual failings. Rather they are the inevitable result of having grown up with homophobia and having had homophobia repeatedly used to undermine the women's movement. Sometimes lesbians do not remember this and turn on individual heterosexual feminists with such cheap shots as "You shouldn't sleep with men, they are the enemy." This is designed only to produce guilt and divisiveness, and to overcompensate for lesbian invisibility by turning the tables on heterosexual feminists and telling them they cannot be real feminists. These oversimplifications are explosions of anger and have no place in political discussions. Feminism asserts the right of all women to make their erotic choices, and this includes choosing men exclusively. Feminism also rejects the hierarchy of sexual practices, and so does not seek to substitute a lesbian priority for heterosexism. The goal of feminism in the area of sexuality is to establish true sexual pluralism, where no one choice is presented as "the norm."

However, having once or twice been faced by dogmatic lesbian chauvinism, sometimes heterosexual feminists retreat and refuse to ask any critical questions about their own views and practices. Being attracted to men is definitely neither unfeminist nor oppressive to lesbians, but since it necessarily fits into the institution of heterosexuality certain questions are helpful. Here are examples of what seem to me to be possible critical questions for heterosexual feminists:
- Do I, even though I am heterosexual, have a "lesbian streak"?
- If so, am I panicked about releasing that energy, and wish lesbians would go away so that I don't have to deal with it?
- Or do I have absolutely no attraction to other women, and think any woman who does must be bizarre?
- Am I afraid a lesbian will try to seduce me?

- Am I secretly hoping a lesbian will seduce me?
- Do I have stereotyped views about lesbian role-playing in relationships? If so, where do those views come from? From actual experience, from the media, from one or two novels or movies?
- Do I assume that all women I meet are heterosexual? Do I think I don't know any lesbians just because none of my friends have explicitly told me they are lesbians?
- If my daughter, sister, or mother came out as a lesbian, would I be embarrassed? If so (and this is only to be expected), do I have any way to develop a more positive attitude and get over my initial anxiety?
- Do I think that having lesbians in the women's movement is a public embarrassment? If so (and this is only to be expected), do I and my heterosexual friends have ways to deal with this? Do we fear guilt by association?
- Can I talk to a lesbian about my fears and concerns? Can I talk to anybody about all these questions?

All these questions are legitimate. Everyone has to struggle with them at some point or another, and this takes time. Heterosexism is so deeply ingrained in us that it takes a concerted effort to overcome it. Being lesbian-positive is not easy, and does not come automatically on joining a women's group, or for that matter on becoming a lesbian.

This means that dialogue is crucial, not just between lesbians and heterosexual women, but among heterosexual women as well. During this dialogue one will probably be faced with questions that have never been asked before, such as "Why am I heterosexual anyway?" Or for lesbians, "Do I secretly think feminists who are not lesbians are second-class feminists?"

The first precondition of dialogue is mutual respect. But the second condition is an awareness that not all sexual choices are created equal. Lesbians are oppressed because of their sexual preference, while heterosexual women acquire certain privileges from society as a result of their sexual preference. Thus, even if we find a lot of common ground and discover that sexual relationships tend to have the same problems, we should not end our investigation with a bland "It's really all the same anyway." Lesbian oppression is not experienced by heterosexual women, and they need to educate themselves about it by talking with lesbians, by reading, and by any other available means.

Once we have mutual respect as well as an awareness of both lesbian oppression and heterosexual privilege, we can move on to discuss our personal concerns and our views about how the women's movement can best fight against heterosexism, which oppresses all independent women, and against the specific oppression of lesbians. This discussion is already taking place in small groups, but it needs to take place more publicly and on a larger scale.

The final goal is a strong women's movement which represents the interests of women of all sexual orientations, and which vocally defends the right of lesbians not only to have private relationships but also to build a visible and public lesbian culture. This culture will of course be of more direct benefit to lesbians. But all women can gain inspiration from seeing the tremendous possibilities that are released when we begin to think about woman-centred eroticism, about woman-oriented culture, about woman-positive politics.

◆

BISEXUALITY: COPING WITH SEXUAL BOUNDARIES

RUTH IS TWENTY-SIX, single, and a strong feminist. While she was attending university on the West Coast, she discovered feminism and almost simultaneously got drawn into a campus feminist group which turned out to be 100 percent lesbian. At first she was a bit shocked. But soon she began to see the world through lesbian eyes, and it did not take long before she was flirting quite openly with Kate, a lesbian whom she thought might be interested in "initiating" her. At first Kate was not receptive, not wanting to get involved with such a greenhorn, but Ruth's persistence paid off. The two women had a passionate affair that lasted eight months—until Kate's ex-lover returned from a year of study in Montreal and wooed Kate back. Ruth was very hurt but she played it cool. A year and two meaningless flings later, she left to go back East. There, living in a small Ontario town, she more or less forgot about her lesbianism, and a few months after moving back she got involved with a male musician. She told him something of her relationship with Kate, but he did not take it seriously, and simply said, "Oh don't worry, it doesn't bother me." So she did not bring it up again. She still subscribed to a couple of lesbian publications, and when they came in the mail she made a point of putting them where her male lover would not see them, without thinking about why.

Lynn is a lesbian, and her friend Laurie, who is a member of the same women's group, is bisexual. When they found that their friendship was quickly acquiring a sexual tinge, they both got a little frightened, and without talking to each other, both pondered a series of questions: how would this affect their work in the group? what about Lynn's ex-lover, who was also in the same group? what about Laurie's male lover? would Laurie know how to manage two completely different relationships in two different worlds? and would Lynn not be too vulnerable?

Laurie talked only to her male lover before entering into the relationship. He accepted it as part of life with a feminist woman. Lynn talked to a few of her friends, who all said, "Maybe a fling would be all right, but if you get in too deep it could be terrible; she'll ditch you for a man when the going gets rough." But Lynn didn't think Laurie was like that. And she had too much of a crush on her to be able to stop herself.

Against all predictions, the relationship not only began but prospered. If there was a women's event on Friday night Lynn and Laurie would go together, and then Laurie would be with her male lover on Saturday while Lynn went out with her other friends. Lynn found herself being closely questioned by all her lesbian friends, who thought this was too good to last.

But it wasn't. It lasted . . . until Lynn herself, whose views on men had undergone quite a drastic change for the better since getting to know (indirectly) Laurie's male lover, began to feel herself getting a crush on a heterosexual male friend. She blocked it for several months, thinking that it was just a phase and that she would get over it; after all, she was quite happy in her relationship with Laurie. But the crush refused to go away. She still spoke as a lesbian, wore lesbian buttons, socialized with her lesbian friends . . . but she had a secret crush on a man. Finally, she decided to tell Laurie about it.

Laurie said, "Well, I'm certainly in no position to prevent you from having other relationships, especially with men. But it's funny you should get a crush on a man now; I have been thinking that I am probably a lesbian, or mostly a lesbian, anyway. . . ."

Ana comes from a working-class Italian family. She is thirty-one and divorced, and has a six-year-old boy. She doesn't want to get seriously involved with anyone, partly because her son had a hard time with the divorce and she thinks it would not be good if he got attached to somebody else only to see that connection vanish. She has had two affairs with women in the last few years, one during a holiday in which she had left her son with his father, and one in a semi-surreptitious manner. She didn't want her son to find out and tell his father about the strange woman in mommy's bedroom. At present Ana is attracted both to men and to women, and knows she could easily get into a relationship with either. But the lesbians she knows are wary of bisexuals; and the men she knows would probably freak out at the thought of her lesbian side, even if they pretended to be cool about it. She feels caught in a net. She hates having to be deceptive; even more, she hates having to *feel* devious and deceptive just because she is bisexual.

◆

The women described above are all in some sense bisexual, but only Ana and Laurie think of themselves in those terms. Ruth might be perceived by some lesbians as a traitor, a "true" lesbian who went straight because it was more convenient. Others might describe her as bisexual or as "really" straight. And as for Lynn and Laurie, who knows.

Underlying these opinions and judgements is the myth that everyone is "really," "deep down," *either* gay *or* straight— except for a very few people who might be allowed to be "really" bisexual. This is the myth that we all have some inner core of sexual truth which exists and persists even while our surface behaviour patterns change. Some people think that this inner core is determined biologically by hormones and genes; others think it is determined by early psychological experiences. Those with a heterosexual bias might tend to believe that a particular person is "really" heterosexual, unless that person protests strongly, while those with a gay bias might tend to think that anyone who is in a gray area is "really" gay. The debate about whether person X is "really" gay or straight, however, fails to question the underlying assumption about the inner sexual core.

The way people use this myth is as follows. If a man who has been having sex with men since age thirteen falls in love with a woman at age thirty-two, this would be "explained" by saying that the man was heterosexual all along but was afraid of women. To go back to our fictional characters, Ruth's experiences could be neatly categorized by saying that she went through a "lesbian phase" under the influence of feminism, and only later realized her "true" heterosexual potential. An alternative but equally mythical explanation would be to say that she found her true nature in lesbianism but then entered a period of "false consciousness" as a result of the failure of her relationship with Kate. The explanations could multiply.

Why are we so intent on assuming an inner core of sexual truth? Why do we have to rewrite our histories and dismiss experiences that were at the time extremely powerful as "just a phase"? Would it not be better to work from the hypothesis that sexual orientation is not a given, like blue eyes or a tendency to gain weight, but is rather subject to profound changes—and is in fact constantly created and recreated—as our sexual and social experiences unfold?

Nobody knows how sexual orientation is in fact determined. One reason for this failure is that almost all research to date has concentrated on finding the "causes" of homosexuality, as if heterosexuality had no cause. Thus, it might be better to work from a hypothesis that allows for both change and positive choices, rather than one which sees people as mere pawns of some hard, fixed core of sexual identity. It is true that there are some people who are exclusively attracted to either one gender or the other, and who from a very tender age felt "pushed" by their exclusive desire. But many other people, and women in particular, experience their own sexual orientation as more fluid. This has to be recognized in any theory of sexual orientation, and clearly the category of bisexuality is an important conceptual tool in this type of analysis.

And yet, the rejection of hetero- and homosexuality as two different species with fixed boundaries does not mean that we should go to the other extreme and dismiss all differences in sexual orientation by blandly saying, "but everyone is bisexual anyway." This statement is often legitimized by reference to the Freudian model of sexual development, which sees early childhood sexuality as the child's pleasure in his/her own body. According to Freud, heterosexuality develops only by means of the resolution of the Oedipus complex. Prior to this, the child does not make gender distinctions in his/her desire, and is primarily focused either on autoerotic activities or on the mother (because she is the primary parent, not because she is female).

This theory can be used to suggest that bisexuals are closer to the innocence of pre-Oedipal childhood than those who have singled out one gender as the sole object of desire. One sometimes hears that bisexuality is superior to both the conformity of exclusive heterosexuality and the narrowness of exclusive homosexuality. In other words, this approach legitimizes bisexuality in the same way that conservative thought legitimizes exclusive heterosexuality, i.e. by reference to a myth of what is "natural." The only difference is that the bisexual myth emphasizes the innocence of early childhood, while the heterosexual myth emphasizes concepts such as "maturity."

The bisexual-as-innocent myth, however, is based on an incorrect reading of Freudian theory. One cannot assume that because babies and young children do not differentiate very much between genders—the significant distinctions are pleasure versus non-pleasure, mother versus absence of mother—therefore adults are in some essential way bisexual. The baby's generalized erotic drives, or "polymorphous perversity" (as Freud called it), is not the same as or even the foundation for adult bisexual behaviour. The baby's erotic drives are not directed toward "men" and "women" as distinct genders, but rather toward autoerotic pleasures such as sucking one's thumb or touching one's genitals, or to the mother as object of desire and source of nurture and pleasure. The infant's sexuality is both pre-genital and pre-gendered.

The bisexual behaviour of adults who choose to eroticize both men and women is the furthest thing from this primeval innocence. Adult bisexuality is both genitally focused (unlike the child's oral, anal and phallic eroticisms) and gender conscious. It is not an innocent, pre-genital eroticization of all bodily experience, but rather involves the selection of properly gendered men and women as objects of desire within the context of fairly rigid rules about what constitutes real sex.

The false analogy between the baby's polymorphous eroticism and the adult's bisexuality has been used to suggest that, far from being indecisive or fickle sexual beings (which is the view of mainstream society), bisexuals are "closer to nature" and are even superior because of their non-exclusivity.

If the myth of a sexual state of nature (in which bisexuals get to play the noble savage) is a useful one in terms of the psychological self-justification of bisexuals, the myth also has certain political uses and consequences. By stressing the alleged "essential" bisexuality of all human beings, heterosexuality and homosexuality tend to appear simply as alternative ways of narrowing down the original sexual drive. They tend to be presented as comparable choices, as "sexual preferences."

The model of "sexual preference," as Adrienne Rich points out in her classic essay "Compulsory Heterosexuality and Lesbian Existence"[1] is problematic mainly because it is based on the liberal myth that one makes one's sexual choices through individual preference. Rich points out that, given the enormous social weight of heterosexism, one cannot accurately describe heterosexuality as merely a personal preference, as though there were not countless social forces pushing one to be heterosexual. People do not generally choose heterosexuality out of a number of equally valid, equally respected lifestyles. Rather, people tend to "naturally" become heterosexual as they become adult sexual beings. By speaking of homosexuality and heterosexuality (and for that matter bisexuality) as "preferences," one is disguising and mystifying the institution that Rich calls "compulsory heterosexuality." As long as certain choices are punished while others are presented as natural, as the norm, it is naive to describe the complicated process of the construction of conformity and/or deviance by reference to a consumer-type notion of personal preference.

To point out that heterosexuality is not accurately described as a "preference" is not to imply that homosexuality or bisexuality, as non-conformist lifestyles, are necessarily "free" choices. As we said earlier, by stepping out of respectability one does not necessarily escape the grasp of the sexual experts; one does not step out of the realm of necessity and into the realm of pure freedom. Many people who are attracted to the "wrong" gender feel *driven* by their own desires, feel compelled to seek homosexual partners, and do not experience their homosexuality as the exercise of freedom. However, even those people who have experienced their homosexual desires as dark forces governing them, rather than as freely chosen paths to self-fulfilment, are forced at some point to define themselves, and ask how and why they have come to have such desires. One may choose to say, "I was born gay," or "I am bisexual because . . ."; but regardless of the answers that we give ourselves, we all have to spend some time thinking about the reasons why we took this particular path, and what the social consequences are. Heterosexuals do not have a comparable experience. Since we all "naturally" grow up to be heterosexual, it is only the deviations that call out for an explanation; the norm appears as natural, and few heterosexual people ever wonder whatever caused them to be heterosexual.

As explained in the previous chapter, society does everything in its power to construct a certain pattern of heterosexual behaviour out of each child's autoerotic and polysexual drives. Sometimes the social forces are for one reason or another ineffectual, and the adolescent or adult "discovers" certain deviant desires in her/himself. Society then does what it can to mould the deviant desires into one of the patterns provided by the experts. If it failed to give you a normal heterosexual identity, it will give you a deviant identity as a homosexual.

It is interesting that although bisexuality, like homosexuality, is just another deviant identity, it also functions as a rejection of the norm/deviance model. People who are bisexual, and not just in a transition between heterosexuality and homosexuality, are people who have resisted both society's first line of attack and its second offensive, i.e. they have resisted both the institution of heterosexuality and of homosexuality. This means that every day they have to make specific choices about how they will appear, with whom they will flirt, what style they will express in clothes and mannerisms.

However, the flexibility and ambiguity inherent in bisexuality do not suffice to allow bisexuals to hover comfortably somewhere "above" the gay/straight split. Nobody can escape the social structures and ideologies that govern both gender formation and sexual-orientation formation, which have created hetero- and homosexuality as the main, institutionalized sexual identities. What bisexuals do is not so much escape the gay/straight split, but rather *manage* it. They are not above the fray, but participate in it by locating themselves at different points in the split according to the circumstances. Bisexuality is best seen not as a completely separate Third Option that removes itself from all the problems of both hetero- and homosexuality, but rather as a choice to combine the two lifestyles, the two erotic preferences, in one way or another.

This view of bisexuality as a combination of the two main sexual identities rather than a separate identity explains how there can be such huge differences among bisexuals. Homosexuals may be very different from each other—the closeted male politician who has secret affairs with boys does not have much in common with the lesbian feminist—but at the very least they all face a common social oppression and a marginalization into gay ghettoes. Bisexuals, on the other hand, do not have a common social experience upon which to build a specific *social* identity, although they do all share the problem of how to manage the gay/straight split and avoid feeling schizophrenic in the process.

Bisexuals who are unaware of the effects of heterosexism, and who see their situation as a purely individual choice with no significant social repercussions, often unwittingly reinforce, or at least go along with, heterosexist practices. If I have two lovers, one male and one female, it will not be easy to keep in mind that the heaps of social approval piled upon my "straight" relationship should be taken with a grain of salt. I will "naturally" tend to keep my lesbian relationship more private, without mentioning it to family and coworkers. I might also be more likely to tolerate faults and selfish habits in a man, because "you know how men are." For all my claims to gender blindness, I will have different expectations from men and from women, and society will treat my two relationships very differently. I might tend to differentiate myself from my lesbian lover, and assume that it will be she who will fight for gay rights, while I nod encouragingly from the sidelines. If I get some tolerance for my lesbian relationship, I might congratulate myself on having tolerant friends, without looking at the historic fight of gays and lesbians to *create* tolerance.

On the other hand, bisexuals who are aware of how gay oppression and heterosexism shape the contours of their own lives are in a good position to challenge these oppressive social forces, even as they make it clear that they are fighting as bisexuals, not as honorary gays or pseudo-gays. Those bisexuals who see themselves as sometimes benefiting from heterosexual privilege and at other times suffering gay oppression, and can see the different consequences of different ways of managing the gay/straight split are also those who tend to take up gay rights as a cause that affects them personally. They are the ones who do not vigorously protest when someone says, "Gee, I saw you going into a gay bar."

However, up until now the gay community has not been at all encouraging or even tolerant of bisexuals who have a commitment to resisting heterosexism and gay oppression. Gay people have traditionally dismissed bisexuals as deceitful, unreliable, and cowardly. This negative view has unfortunately been confirmed by the existence of many bisexuals who maintain a public heterosexual image while indulging in gay relationships in private, thus escaping gay oppression in a way that gay people can never do. Gay people do have a right to demand that bisexuals do not fall into the easy trap of being publicly straight and privately gay. However, there are now bisexuals, especially feminist women, who are resisting that traditional easy approach and who are increasingly willing to be public about their gay side. They have to be welcomed and treated with respect for their sexual choice. Gay people have to stop assuming that everyone who is bisexual is simply either afraid of coming out or is in transition to being fully gay. The transition theory assumes that those who call themselves bisexual are "really" gay, and this is as much an error as the belief that everyone is "really" bisexual. Both rely on the assumption that sexual orientation is an inner essence, an assumption known as "essentialism."

Because of our society's firmly entrenched belief in sexual essentialism, we are all more or less uncomfortable with people who are sexually ambiguous. We insist that everyone have a fixed gender identity and a fixed sexual orientation. When we see someone in the street and we cannot tell if it is a man or a woman, we get uneasy and go out of our way to get a second look. We do not rest until we have determined the correct gender of this person (who is otherwise completely unimportant to us). Now, sexual orientation is not as visible on a person as gender, but we all derive a certain satisfaction from investigating people's sexual identities and proceeding to label them as X or Y. Bisexuality is threatening partly because it seems to challenge our classification system, thus putting into question fundamental notions about sexuality and gender. Thus, even if some traditional bisexual behaviour patterns are questionable, and even though there is no such thing as an institutionalized bisexuality comparable to hetero- and homosexuality, I still think it is important to give sexual ambiguity a place in the sun of radical sexual thought. In other words, even though I share some of the gay skepticism about bisexuality, and am concerned to see bisexuals take a more active role in challenging heterosexism, I am also critical of the dogmatic view—found as much among gay people as among straight people—that bisexuals are inherently indecisive and immature. If the goals of feminism and gay liberation include the abolition of the gay/straight split, and its replacement by a social system which does not label and categorize people according to whom they are attracted, then bisexuality is an important part of the challenge to the status quo. Its role could involve vindicating and affirming sexual ambiguity, in a world which is presently extremely uncomfortable with any ambiguity. Bisexuality defies the experts' attempts to classify everything as either male or female, normal or deviant, good or bad.

One day over lunch, a bisexual friend was lamenting the fact that she seemed to be constantly faced with ethical and political dilemmas, and she reflected on the plight of bisexual women who are forever being judged and scrutinized. I nodded sympathetically, and tried to tell her not to worry about how she was presenting herself in the women's movement, or about whether lesbians would be offended if she called herself a lesbian in order to share lesbian oppression and take responsibility for it. She was, I thought, an honest and thoughtful person, so I told her, "trust your political intuition, don't be so introspective, there'll always be somebody who criticizes you no matter what you do."

The next day I had dinner with a lesbian friend who has been badly burned by bisexual women twice. Both of these bisexual women were self-consciously attractive and charismatic. They both seemed at first interested in a serious relationship, but in the end discarded her, or rather, treated her as a second-class lover. As she recounted the experiences for my benefit, I thought, "Maybe I should not have been so understanding yesterday—you never know what will happen if you tell bisexual women to just trust their political and ethical intuition."

I later decided that the two experiences—that of my bisexual friend intent on being responsible, and that of my lesbian friend burned by bisexual women—were qualitatively different, and there was little point in putting them both in the bisexual file. What was at issue in my lesbian friend's unhappy experience was not her lovers' eroticization of men as well as women, but rather the way they used their access to men (and therefore to status) against her and against the relationship. It is not that their heartlessness derives from their bisexuality. Rather, bisexuality offered their selfishness ample ground to exercise itself.

By contrast, my bisexual friend was keenly aware of the potential power imbalance inherent in a relationship between a bisexual and a lesbian, and she was trying to find ways to counteract and subvert that potential. She was, in other words, counteracting the privilege she had acquired in her heterosexual life. This is why she wanted to publicly identify with lesbians—although she was understandably intimidated by the lesbian feminist heavies who had denounced her as "not a real lesbian." I could see why some lesbians might feel uncomfortable with women who identify as lesbians without being fully integrated into lesbian life; but in my opinion, those lesbians are being dogmatic and are too zealously guarding the boundaries of lesbianism. They are victims of society's general tendency to feel uncomfortable with ambiguity.

Bisexuality does not exist as either a social institution or a psychological "truth." It only exists as a catch-all term for different erotic and social patterns whose common ground is an attempt to combine homo- and heterosexuality in a variety of ways. The term "bisexual," then, merely tells us that someone can or does eroticize both men and women. It does not tell us anything about the morality or politics of that person. The decisions that inevitably have to be made about how to manage one's sexual life and one's social image will be based on extraneous factors (such as commitment to feminism).

However, there is one important way in which bisexuality plays a role in the struggle for a society free from sharp gender and sexual orientation boundaries. This lies in the implicit challenge to notions of essential and static sexual identities. Even those people who define themselves as "definitely gay" or "definitely straight" are often in the position of having to admit to desires that do not fit their current social identity—the autobiographical anecdotes I presented in the chapter on heterosexuality are just one example of this. And in this sense it would be a great boon to all of us if there were more social space for self-defined bisexuals. This would mean that we would all be a little freer from exclusivist and essentialist definitions. Of course, because our society is rigidly gendered and is heterosexist in structure, it would be utopian to imagine that bisexuality could exist in a haven beyond gender and beyond gay oppression. But even a bisexuality with all the contradictions imposed on it by our society can help to challenge the sexual status quo. Contradictions, after all, are the moving force of history.

◆

CHAPTER FIVE

PORNOGRAPHY: NOT FOR MEN ONLY

PORNOGRAPHY IS one of the hot issues of the eighties, both in the women's movement and elsewhere in society such as police departments and fundamentalist churches. For feminists, the porn debate is a many-headed beast, involving different aspects of our analysis of society. To discuss porn is to raise our consciousness about violence against women. It is also to wonder at the seeming perversity of male sexual fantasies, and thus to cast doubts on the character of "normal" heterosexuality. Furthermore, some studies appear to show that violent porn actually leads to an increase in men's aggressive attitudes toward women. While it has not been shown that this attitudinal change causes rapes or assaults that would not otherwise have taken place, the effects on men and indirectly on women are clearly negative.

Perhaps more importantly, whether or not violent porn actually causes violence, women do feel violated by its imagery. Andrea Dworkin has been the most prominent feminist to give voice to those feelings of violation. While most other feminists reject her simplistic equation of patriarchal power and porn, and many criticize her pro-censorship views as far too sweeping, the fact is that women do feel attacked and made vulnerable by images of bound and gagged women.

These feelings of violation, and not so much statistics about levels of aggressiveness in males, constitute the ground on which the by now famous censorship debate is taking place. Feminists and non-feminists alike have been awakened to what it is that men are consuming, and are calling on the state to control or even ban images which appear to legitimize or encourage male sexual violence.

In the meantime, other women have countered that we are being short-sighted if we focus only on violent porn. It can be argued that pornography is not an isolated form of woman-hatred that can be controlled or suppressed, but is rather a more glaring example than usual of how the mass media portray women and relations between men and women. If we accept this (and I do) then it follows that we have to question not just porn but also the more innocuous representations found in advertising, in Hollywood films, and in television culture, all of which tend to portray women as the contented slaves of male desire. To suppress a few pictures or cut a few seconds from a movie does not help to make the world safer for women; rather, censoring certain bits and pieces out of the huge production of the mass media can lull us into a false sense of security.

I will return to the censorship question at the end of the chapter, after the discussions of what pornography is and what purpose it serves in our society. For now suffice it to say that the "porn question" is actually many questions. It involves the issue of male sexual and non-sexual violence; the problem of masculine sexuality and masculine desire; the relationship of women to forms of culture seldom recognized as pornographic; the political question of how far feminists can expect the government and the police to behave in our interests; and also the whole problem of the dehumanized portrayal of women in the mass media. No wonder we argue about porn for hours!

It makes sense to tackle these various issues one by one, using both feminist theory and critical studies of the mass media. We cannot just explode in anger against male violence and let our anger be a substitute for reason. We do need to feel how angry we are and how angry we have been for years without even knowing it. But then what? When we are in a rage, our rage is all too easily exploited and manipulated by self-appointed censors and moral policemen who want to be given a mandate to "protect" and hide us under their ample patriarchal wings. For instance, Toronto mayor Art Eggleton, in a submission to the Canadian federal government's Fraser Commission on Pornography and Prostitution of February 1984, cynically used women's anger about porn in order to further his own law-and-order interests. He promised an all-out crackdown not just on pornography but on what he called "the double-headed beast of pornography and prostitution."

Victorian imagery of double-headed beasts aside, one wonders at the logical sleight-of-hand involved in using a few feminist phrases to launch an attack on prostitutes, calling for stricter laws to allow the police to make more arrests. In laws concerning prostitution and pornography as in so many other forms of patriarchal ideology and practice, protection and oppression are but two sides of the same coin. Since the nineteenth century, when "protective" legislation was used to ban women from certain industrial jobs under the pretext that women needed special protection from physical and moral hazards, the rhetoric of protection of women has often been used to protect male privilege and to disempower women.

In this chapter I do not want to go through the arguments about whether or not porn causes men to be more violent toward women than they "normally" are. The studies which make this claim are in any case inconclusive. But more importantly, the aggression research studies avoid the crucial question of pornography's effect on us, on women. We are not simply billiard balls waiting to be hit by men who have in turn been hit by images of women in chains. The social world cannot be adequately studied from a perspective that sees action and motivation as reducible to the stimulus-response model of behaviourist psychology. And, even if this model did to some extent apply to male consumers of violent porn, it would not follow that women are affected only insofar as men act out their fantasies on us. We are intelligent human beings, not passive victims, and we are directly affected by the culture around us. We have something to say on the question of images of women, regardless of how they affect men.

An innovative approach is required in studying women's relation to pornography. We cannot look at porn as a bad thing out there that men buy and then "act out." We have to see pornography as an *element* that runs throughout our whole culture. Rather than try to isolate porn as a particular object, it might be more useful to speak about "the pornographic" as an aspect of many apparently harmless films, books, and magazines. When we stop worrying about defining porn narrowly enough so that only the worst stuff comes under legal scrutiny, and begin to define it broadly enough to encompass those aspects of mass culture that glamourize the subjection of women, then we will have learned something not just about male lust but also about women's own fantasies and desires. These are to a large extent constructed by traditional feminine culture embodying the same power relations that we see expressed in violent porn.

The effect of pornography on women will be the main focus of this chapter. I put the discussion in the context of a definition of pornography that encompasses not only male-oriented erotic literature but also those mass-produced cultural products that are addressed to women and which glamourize and eroticize their subordination. At the end of the chapter, I will use the insights gained by this unorthodox approach to make a few recommendations for political action against violent heterosexual male pornography.

DEFINING PORNOGRAPHY

Pornography is a collection of images and texts, representations which have something in common. Defining that "something" is the subject of a great deal of discussion. However, before we can try to define pornographic content we need some idea of how to analyze and classify *representations* in general.

There are many types of representations in our culture, such as avant-garde visual art, soap operas, Western films, romance novels, symphonies, love songs, housewife magazines, and detective novels. These are just a few of the many genres available to us mostly through mass-produced cultural industries. Just as it is sometimes difficult to establish whether a particular popular song is "country and western" or "pop," or whether a particular popular novel is a detective story or a spy thriller, it is difficult to know exactly what is or is not pornography. *Penthouse* is pornography, more or less by definition, but what about D.H. Lawrence's novels? Or gay male magazines containing erotic photos? Or sex manuals? Or novels written by women about women who have sex frequently? Or television commercials featuring scantily clad blondes draped over a household appliance or a car?

The problem is that there are no litmus tests for what is or is not pornography. For pornography is not a natural object that can be classified, like a particular species of butterfly, but rather a complex cultural *process*. It is a process because it necessarily establishes, and is established by, a particular set of relations between producer and consumer, between consumer and his/her social context, and between the social context and the producer. Pornography does not drop from heaven onto our local corner-store shelves. It is first *produced* by certain people who relate to one another via the pornography industry; it is then *consumed* by customers who buy porn in the expectation of being aroused; and finally, porn derives most of its meaning and significance from the *social context* in which it exists.

Elsewhere I have analyzed in more detail the production and consumption dimensions of pornography. I have commented on the inadequacy of measures that seek merely to interfere either with production (e.g. prior censorship) or with consumption (e.g. bylaws regulating sales), without a broader understanding of the process involved in the creation both of porn itself and of the "porn consumer."[1] Here I would like to focus mainly on social context, partly because it has been almost completely neglected in feminist discussions and partly because it is the element most relevant to our question regarding the impact of pornography on women.

When we look at a *Playboy* centrefold we generally see a young white woman with a flawless body; she is either sitting or reclining, her genital area is exposed in a purposeful manner and is usually in the centre of the picture. In itself, the picture does not have very much meaning. We supply most of the meaning ourselves, from our experience of living in a sexist, ageist and racist society, and from our general knowledge of what *Playboy* is and what is expected of the viewer. We know from sources outside the magazine that it is not coincidental that the woman in the picture is young, slim, white, and helpless-looking. We know from our own experience that the photo was created for a male audience and that when a man looks at it he will react in certain specified ways. He will not merely glance at the photo as he would at a landscape or a family photograph; he will gaze intently, stare at, and *possess* that woman with his eyes. We also know, from our knowledge of how capitalism works, that the purpose of the publication is not to celebrate the female body but rather to use female bodies to make profits. Thus, we use our knowledge of both the production and the consumption processes involved in pornography to interpret the picture and ascribe to it a meaning.

Furthermore, we are informed about the usual relations between men and women in our society, and that information is what produces the feelings we experience when looking at the otherwise harmless photo. We feel embarrassed for the model because we know that her apparent naive innocence is a deception designed to heighten the male's pleasure in conquering the pictured body. We feel angry at men, both those who make money from the photo and those who spend money on it. We feel vulnerable and at risk. But it is not the picture itself which creates these feelings. If men never raped women in real life, the same picture would not have the same power to make us feel violated.

A different, negative example. One could imagine writing a radical feminist sci-fi story in which men were portrayed as stupid creatures only good for sex and reproduction. And yet, even if it offended men, such a story could not make them feel violated, threatened, or at risk, since reality would still be firmly in patriarchal hands. Because women do not have the social power to subdue, exploit, or marginalize men, feminist fantasies of a matriarchal world can never have the same social significance and the same impact on men as pornography does on women. Men may dislike matriarchal fantasies, but no fantasy can succeed in making them afraid to walk the streets alone at night for fear of being attacked by a gang of women.

Thus, our experience in a sexist society helps in a very important way to determine how we will interpret representations of sex and gender. The very meaning of representation is largely determined by its social context. For instance, a photo of a woman kneeling down to perform fellatio on a man has a very different social meaning than a picture of a man kneeling to perform cunnilingus on a woman. The first picture implies subordination, while the second merely implies that a man is giving a woman pleasure. The difference in the connotations is not due to anything in the photos themselves, but rather to the "usual" connotations of women's bodies versus men's bodies.

The meaning of a particular representation is further specified by the context in which the representation appears. If we are watching a pornographic film, a close-up shot of a peach cut in half will have sexual connotations, whereas the same shot would not arouse anybody if it were part of a food advertisement. The following example will make this point clearer.

The June 1985 issue of *Forum*, a soft-core porn magazine published by *Penthouse* and containing only articles and textual erotic fantasies, carried a feature enticingly entitled "Sex Lives of Lesbian Nuns." The piece consisted of a series of excerpts from a book of personal stories by nuns and ex-nuns who had either had lesbian love affairs in the convent, usually with little or no genital sex, or who had come out as lesbians after leaving the convent. The book was edited by two lesbian ex-nuns and published by the U.S. lesbian feminist press Naiad. The sale of excerpt rights to *Forum* was widely denounced by lesbian feminists, including some of the ex-nuns who had contributed their personal accounts to the book on the understanding that it was going to be published by a small feminist press and would be sold as a feminist product to a feminist audience. They were horrified to see their lives turned into pornography.[2]

This is not the place to explore the complicated ethical and legal questions regarding the sale of other people's words. We are only concerned with how this sale of feminist texts to a porn outfit sheds light on the problem of defining pornography. The reader of the book approaches it as a lesbian feminist text, which deals specifically with Catholic experiences and asks many questions about spirituality, bonding between women, sexuality and guilt, repression, and the racial and class contradictions between women in convents. The erotic passages are few and far between: even women who were aware of their lesbianism while they were nuns seldom had sex. Either through ignorance, shame, or because of the vow of chastity, sexual pleasure was generally limited to kissing and mild fondling. Even in the excerpts published in *Forum*, which were culled for their presumed erotic value, there are few explicit descriptions of sexual pleasure. There are, however, a great many descriptions of sexual guilt, and undoubtedly some readers experience pleasure when reading about sexual guilt.

In the context of *Forum* sexual guilt is pornographic. Whereas in the book the descriptions of guilt serve to illuminate how Catholicism works, and so educate the reader about a particular segment of the lesbian community, in *Forum* the same words come across as pornographic clichés. Convents, Mother Superiors, male confessors, novice mistresses, penances, self-mortification and all the other elements of Catholic life have not coincidentally been part of the stock in trade of pornographers since the Marquis de Sade.

This shift in meaning of the autobiographical elements illustrates the importance of context for defining what is or is not pornography. A story which comes across as a moving personal account of a woman discovering her own sexuality in a Catholic environment suddenly turns into a pornographic cliché, merely because it was taken out of a lesbian feminist context and published in a pornographic one.

The example just mentioned shows that one cannot always decide what is or is not pornography merely by looking at the picture or text in question. This decision involves such other factors as context and mode of production and consumption. Because of the difficulties involved in isolating a specific set of representations and labelling them "pornographic" regardless of purpose, use and context, it might be more useful to speak of pornographic elements in our culture. These elements are present together in most mass-produced films and magazines designed explicitly by the producers as "porn." But each element or even several at once are also found in other cultural genres.

Thus far feminist analyses of porn have tended to focus only on male sexual violence against women. Important as this one component is, there are others which are equally essential in the constitution of pornography as a cultural genre. Looking at a representative sample of soft-core porn magazines (which have much larger circulations than hard-core ones, and are bought by significant numbers of women[3]) I was able to distinguish three main elements almost invariably found in the magazine as a whole, though not necessarily in each article or photo spread.

(1) *The portrayal of men's social and physical power over women as sexy.* This includes eroticizing guns, uniforms, and other symbols of male power, most notably wealth. By contrast, women are eroticized in their powerlessness, as indicated by their extreme youth, physical vulnerability, stance and facial expression. For men, power equals sexiness, whereas for women the equation is reversed. A woman millionaire, a woman Prime Minister, a woman athlete—all these women have to prove they are feminine and desirable to men, because the immediate assumption is that their power renders them masculine or sexless. (cf. the endless discussions by sports writers about whether or not this or that woman athlete is truly feminine. East European athletes are especially suspect because in their societies the use of make-up, fancy haircuts, jewelry, etc. is not as encouraged as in consumer capitalist societies.)

(2) *The depiction of aggression, both sexual and non-sexual, as the inevitable result of power imbalances.* That is, the impression is created that those who have power will tend to abuse it and dominate others. This belief is by no means unique to pornography, but it is used by the producers of porn to signal certain things. For instance, given what we know about gender and race relations, when a pornographic magazine shows us a picture of white cowboys standing beside Indian women, we know the next picture will show the rape or at least the seduction of the Indian women. The pornographer does not have to depict the actual rape; we fill in the blanks ourselves.

This conception of power is found in almost all popular culture, from Westerns to war movies, from Gothic romances to spy thrillers. But in pornography it plays the specific role of equating women's sexual availability with an immediate danger of rape and even murder. While business magazines suggest it is men's nature to forsake all for the sake of profits, pornography assumes that men will abuse or at the very least fuck women whenever they can. Once we have learned this belief, it does not have to be spelled out each time it is used. We can be given only a picture of a sexually aroused male, and we will once more fill in the blanks and assume that any woman in his vicinity is in danger.

(3) *The undermining of social barriers and conventions by the relentless power of sex.* Pornography tends to use stereotyped social roles rather than fully developed characters. We are not presented with such fictional individuals as Anna Karenina or Madame Bovary, but only with such cardboard characters as the bored housewife, the sexy milkman, the nymphet, the young male jock, and the innocent co-ed. Many of these roles would, in real life, put a distance between one person and another. For instance, the milkman has a specific job to do, and the housewife presumably has an allegiance to her husband and is not normally available to other men. But pornography sees its role as demolishing all social barriers by connecting, through sex, people who are generally kept separate by society's rules. We know this about pornography, so when we begin to read a story about a high school girl and her teacher we immediately expect the usual barrier between teacher and young student to be overcome by mutual lust. Similarly, if a woman is presented as unavailable to men (most commonly the nun and the lesbian) we again expect to see this apparent unavailability denied as sex bursts through the boundaries. Hence, the description of a woman as either a lesbian or a nun will function in the pornographic code as a signal indicating that this woman poses a particular challenge to the male subject. So, in the pornographic context the very word "lesbian" acts as a stimulus to male desire.

This undermining of social distinctions by the power of passion is not necessarily sexist. It is the main ingredient of erotic literature of any kind, from highbrow novels to women's romances. Usually however it is expressed within a sexist context. But the idea of sex as the great leveller which eliminates all social conventions is not per se a patriarchal one.

If this third aspect of pornography is also found in erotic representations that few people would call pornographic, the first two aspects, the most objectionable from a feminist perspective, are also found in many other cultural forms. As for the first, the eroticization of men's domination and women's subordination, a look at any mass-market women's magazine will reveal what sort of man is portrayed as most sexually desirable: men who are physically strong, macho-looking, and who hold a good deal of social power. Doctors, lawyers, professional athletes, executives—these are the men that we are taught to fantasize about, to desire.

We have only to listen to sociobiologists talk about "innate" male aggression and the value of competitiveness and jealousy to see that the second element, the depiction of aggression resulting inevitably from power imbalances, is not unique to pornography. Now, it is true that in our competitive society everyone is put in the position of having to elbow their way to the top. Power is generally used against others rather than with them. However, as we discussed in chapter one, this is not necessarily inherent in human nature. Those who portray power in this way are invoking the nebulous concept of "human nature" in order to justify present social arrangements. I do not see why we should assume that because women are usually physically weaker than men, we will forever have to live in fear of being assaulted. There are a lot of very strong women on my soccer team, and it would never occur to them to use their collective strength to intimidate or assault weaker human beings. Surely it is society, not nature, which tells men that women are potential victims of their violence.

In summary, there are indeed pernicious messages contained in, but not unique to, pornography. They are ideological elements found in many mass-produced cultural products. Moreover, the messages cannot be summarized by, or limited to, the legitimation of male violence against women. The depiction of power as necessarily based on, and resulting in, competition and aggression does not only legitimize and promote male domination. It also legitimizes class exploitation, racism and war, and makes them seem somehow "natural."

To focus only on sexual domination is a narrow perspective, and one which white middle-class women might tend to take because they are not subject to other forms of domination. But a feminism which is more broadly based and which takes into account the experience of women of colour and women in the Third World will have to take a serious look at the glamourization of racism and capitalism, not just the glamourization of sexual subordination. Pornography often eroticizes several forms of domination at once. Consider, for example, the cliché scenes about white male explorers coming upon a "primitive" society whose women are portrayed as "natural" sex objects free of the inhibitions of white Protestant ladies.

Pornography eroticizes social domination in general. A picture that presents a white British army officer flogging an Indian soldier (cf. the television series *The Jewel and the Crown*) is in my mind pornographic, even though there are no women involved. The picture has a definite sexual overtone which helps to disguise the real nature of British imperialism, in the same way that *Penthouse* photos of women begging to be penetrated help to disguise the real nature of sexism.

The eroticization of social domination is also an element in advertising, women's magazines, and the mainstream media in general. Soap operas, for instance, probably do more than any other medium to teach women to see wealth and power as erotic. Devotees of *Dallas* know that the glamorous women in the show might make a mistake and fall in love with the "wrong" man. But they would never fall in love with a man of the wrong class or race. The invisibility of black people, of the Chicano population, and of the workers who produce the Ewing millions is a statement in itself. Because these people are outside the world of wealth, they are also outside the realm of significant sexual intrigue.

Pornography is not an aberration in an otherwise civilized and egalitarian culture. It is part and parcel of the cultural industry that has given us sexist advertising, racist war movies, and classist soap operas. My contention here is that its specific role in this cultural industry is to eroticize social domination, and most notably gender domination.

SELF-COERCION AND THE DENIAL OF EROTIC POWER

In trying to isolate the pornographic element in our culture, feminist writers and lawyers have tended to separate violent porn from all other sexual representations and all other portrayals of women. This is a disservice to the women's movement. The early critiques of porn begun in the late sixties were undertaken as part of a wider critique that included advertising images and such practices as beauty pageants. The protest was not just against images of violence, but against any images that portrayed women as stupid and only good for fucking. It is very unfortunate that this connection has taken a back seat to the question of violence in the current debates. Even if violent porn is what angers women most, it is not necessarily the cultural form most dangerous to our own emotional and sexual development. No woman sees the anonymous models portrayed as victims of male violence as role models. But who among us is not influenced by the equally pernicious messages that tell us to be thin, to wear tight jeans, to be attractive to men? I am not convinced that porn increases violence against women, but what about the self-inflicted violence many women suffer as a result of male-oriented images of beauty and desirability? Women destroy their tendons by wearing high heels, spoil their eating habits by alternating binging and dieting, and ruin their emotional health by constantly worrying about their looks.

It would indeed be convenient if all the oppression and violence women suffer were located out there in the pornography industry. But it is not. We degrade and coerce ourselves as soon as we internalize the dictates of sexism, and there is no law or censor board in the world that can protect us against that. The only way that we can, in the long term, overthrow the system which eroticizes and legitimizes domination by making it glamorous and sexy is to empower ourselves, and this includes sexual self-determination and empowerment. Many of the feminists who are concerned about pornography are neglecting to make this necessary connection, and are in some ways telling us to retreat into traditional feminine roles. Let me explain.

The anti-porn film *Not A Love Story*, produced by the Canadian National Film Board, assaults the audience's senses with footage of the seedier corners of New York's sex industry and with clips of extremely violent porn films. This assault is, much to the viewer's relief, periodically broken by interviews with noted anti-porn theorists Robin Morgan and Susan Griffin. They are portrayed as eminently "nice" women—unlike those seen working in the sex industry—and Morgan is even interviewed in the admiring company of her husband and son. Morgan's family appears (and is deliberately presented by both Morgan and the interviewer) as the polar opposite of pornography: the Holy Family.[4] Apart from the rampant heterosexism of the scene—why should feminist theory have to be validated by the exhibition of the theorist's husband and son? —the effect of the juxtaposition of "holy family" and "bad pornography" is to suggest that those two institutions are opposites and mutually exclusive. But the feminist tradition has always emphasized the necessary connection between the madonna and the whore, the wife and the mistress, the mother and the sex worker. Prostitution and respectable marriage, as nineteenth century feminists pointed out, exist side by side and reinforce each other. To separate the virtuous mother/wife from the stripper and the hooker, assigning to the former the role of "analyzing" the latter, is to fall into the patriarchal trick of isolating women from each other. Patriarchal values have historically oppressed both the wife and the slut, the mother and the stripper. These values are not radically challenged by Robin Morgan's tearful account of the struggles she has gone through with her husband to maintain their relationship in the face of the hostile world of porn and violence. She dismisses "promiscuity" as inherently male (thus passing judgement on women who do not share her commitment to monogamous heterosexuality) and puts forward an essentially middle-class model of "working at one's relationship" as the answer to the problems posed by violent porn.

Clearly, women who live with men have to undergo many struggles to equalize and sustain their relationships. But there is no reason to glorify this particular struggle and present it as "the feminist solution." Many women do not have cooperative husbands or partners with whom they struggle. Is the sexuality of those women therefore outside the purview of real feminism? If all feminist theory has to offer women is a struggling relationship, with sexual pleasure left unmentioned as though it were men's exclusive concern, how is this a challenge to femininity? Pleasure and lust are indeed women's concerns, feminist concerns, and they must be taken into account in any project to replace the pornographic code by woman-positive (and sex-positive) cultural codes.

Susan Griffin, for her part, is presented by the film as the stereotypical image of Natural Womanhood. Blonde, healthy, and wearing no make-up, she sits in bright sunlight surrounded by plants. She waxes mystical about all the values of which women are the true custodians: nurturing, affection, morality. If masculine sexuality equals porn, then feminine sexuality must equal the opposite of porn, i.e. love, affection, "relation-ships," spirituality. Again we have traditional feminine values being prescribed as the remedy for porn, as though pornography and traditional femininity were not two sides of the same sexist stereotype coin.

If we object to women being depicted as "sluts," surely the feminist response is not to flee into the opposite stereotype and proclaim our virtuousness and innocence. If we object to the way men express their sexuality because they tend to think of us as objects to be owned, the alternative is not to pretend that we women have never longed to possess another's body.[5] If we want to tell men that sex is not about domination, we should not tell women that sex is always about nurturing and love. If we object to male partners sleeping around in an irresponsible manner, the solution is not to suggest that all women are by nature monogamous. There are two poles to the double stan-dard, and we cannot claim to be undermining patriarchy if we criticize only the male pole and reinforce the feminine end of the deal. We have to deny both sides of the double standard. We have to acknowledge that the myth of the madonna is as false as the myth of the whore, and that both myths form a single whole. It is not necessary to use clichéd notions of nur-turing love in our solution to the problem of violent, aggres-sive sex: we could try thinking about good sex instead.

By rejecting violent sex, some feminists express a more gen-eral fear of all erotic power. An example of this is found in a brief submitted to the Fraser Commission on Prostitution and Pornography. This document is written by a group of femin-ist lawyers called the Toronto Area Caucus of Women and the Law. Most of the brief is devoted to the search for a fairly narrow definition of violent pornography, for the purposes of criminalizing it. But at one point in the paper they state that although only explicitly violent forms of pornography should be controlled by the government, any "portrayal of power over another human being for the purpose of sexually stimulating the viewer" is per se pornographic.

The conclusion that these women fail to draw is that any realistic representation of "normal" heterosexuality would by their definition be pornographic. A photo showing a wealthy businessman with an adoring and financially dependent woman at his side would be pornographic, since the male viewer would be stimulated by the thought that money buys both sex and adoration.

Even more significantly, a great deal of women's popular literature, and indeed any novel in which people are driven by a strong sexual obsession, would also be deemed pornographic.

THE EROTICIZATION OF DOMINATION IN FORMULA ROMANCE

If we use the distinction that I drew earlier between *power* and *domination*, we would see that it is true indeed that women's popular romances are pornographic, not because they eroticize power, but because they eroticize domination. There are many novels written by women which eroticize the power that one person has over the other. One individual falls in love with, or is sexually obsessed by another, and is therefore under his/her power. But this power does not correspond with, and is not reinforced by socially structured domination. On the other hand, the paperback romances that so many women consume are full of depictions of *domination* as sexy. It is not the accidental sexual power of one individual over another that is the focus of the story, but rather the eroticized domination of those who rule over those who are ruled. This is not just a matter of eroticizing the traditional imbalance between the sexes; class inequality is eroticized as well. The silver-haired boss is often the prime object of the secretary's desire, and his Rolls and luxurious house are always described in loving detail and presented as constituents of the man's sexual appeal. The man usually abuses his power and exercises domination by sexually harassing the heroine, by being physically aggressive, and/or by threatening to fire her. But all these acts of domination are presented as inherently sexy. These incidents always fuel the flames of the younger woman's desire, even though they simultaneously trigger danger signals in her mind.

The women of these romances are no wimps; they want their independence—up to a point. They work outside the home, they never have parents or other authority figures, and they do not necessarily fall for the first man who flatters them. But the men they do fall for are always more socially powerful than they. The male heroes are white and middle-class; they are also older than the heroines, often a lot older.

The only difference between the hero and the villain (there's invariably a villain) is that the villain actually tries to carry out his threats to rape the heroine or bring her to ruin, while the hero always stops at the last minute. The hero falls in love at some point late in the book, and this acts as a check on his otherwise "natural" impulses to abuse women sexually, emotionally and even financially. In a Silhouette romance, the hero meets the heroine when they talk in his office about a possible contract. He bluntly suggests a dinner date, implying the contract depends on her accepting the date. The heroine is angered at his presumption and his overt use of the economic power he has over her, but she is also sexually flattered. The hero's exercise of gender and class domination is both threatening and intriguing to the young heroine. She is trying hard to become an independent businesswoman, but she secretly yearns to give up control to a stronger being. The discouragements inherent in women's economic struggles are mystified by being "translated" into sexual language. The heroine is presented not as the victim of an unjust economic system, but as a trembling female body yearning to be engulfed by the power of the male.

The real-life problems inherent in women's economic inferiority are simultaneously ignored and glamourized. Male economic power and women's lack of economic power are both given a sexual gloss. Sexual attraction is portrayed as being embedded in unequal socio-economic relations between the sexes, and financial inequality is sexualized. The marriage at the end of every book is presented as the resolution of all contradictions. Yet what the marriage actually does is institutionalize the inequality. Through marriage the woman will have access to her husband's wealth and power, but she will continue to be the inferior partner.

Thus it is not coincidental that the only sexuality the heroines appear to have consists of passive eroticism. Because of the strong links between socio-economic inequality and eroticism, to allow women an active sexuality would involve revolutionizing a lot more than the bedroom. It would be impossible to equalize the sexual roles in formula romances without challenging the social roles.

To further explore this point, let us quote some typical passages:

> Women always looked at Alex Brent like that . . . His lean, hard body held a menacing sexuality, an implicit threat of sexual violence which attracted women like iron filings to a magnet.

and

> He had hated her with a burning intensity only because he had loved her so deeply. His hatred was as strong as his love. And that was what made her mind up for her. When a man loves you as much as that, she reasoned happily, how can you turn him down?

Now, when one reverses the pronouns in these passages, substituting "he" for "she" and "men" for "women," one does not create an image of a powerful, sexually assertive woman to whom men are attracted like iron filings to a magnet. Rather, the effect is to create a ridiculous piece of prose portraying women as evil witches. No woman would be able to identify with those images of female desire and be turned on by them.

Because active sexuality is equated with domination or the abuse of institutionalized power it is impossible to depict women's active sexual desire without turning the women into monstrous super-bitches. There is no room either for a passive eroticism that is not powerless, or for an active eroticism that is not "menacing" or based on the "implicit threat of sexual violence." Both poles of the dynamic of erotic power have been hopelessly mired in gender stereotypes, and in turn these have been affixed to the social structure of patriarchal capitalism. Women's passive eroticism is described in a distorted and partial way when it is made synonymous with social subordination and personal powerlessness. And women's active eroticism cannot be described at all, except as the evil doings of a crazed nymphomaniac.

Patriarchal ideology is woven into the very language used to describe sexual arousal and satisfaction. Women do not lust after a man, they "tremble," "quiver," "shudder," and display other Jello-like behaviour. Men, by contrast, do not want pleasure as much as they want to dominate. Even an ordinary kiss can become a sadistic tool to convey not passion but "punishment," "He crushed her roughly closer, and as she lifted her chin to protest, drove his mouth down on hers in a kiss that explained everything without words. It was a punishment in itself. . . ."

Popular erotic literature written for women fails them at a sexual level precisely because it fails to challenge the social status quo. It takes social relations for granted and portrays sexual power as belonging exclusively to powerful men. It portrays women's desire as purely passive, as the desire to be dominated and subdued and "rescued" from the hassles of trying to become an independent and financially secure woman. No wonder marriage is invariably the resolution of all contradictions and tensions in the plot. Traditional marriage is the only social means of reconciling male domination with women's protection. It is the only institution that allows women to give in to their sexual desire without being cast into the fringes of society. The institution of marriage tames the male "impulse" to dominate women, or rather channels it into a monogamous and publicly accountable relationship. This provides safety for women while allowing men unlimited access to one female.

Of course this is not necessarily true in reality. For a lot of women marriage is neither sexually pleasurable nor physically safe. But we are speaking about the institution and the ideology of marriage, and paperback romances are concerned with the ideology, not the reality. The ideology is that men are dangerous, and so women can only "let go" with their husbands, because only their husbands have a duty to take care of them after they have fucked them. Only in marriage is the male urge to possess somewhat countered by a duty to protect. One could thus convincingly argue that the view of men presented in formula romances is much more pessimistic and bleak, and hence more anti-male, than the images of men presented in feminist fiction.

In several ways, then, women's popular fiction not only resembles pornography but actually is pornographic. There is an eroticization not only of male sexual power but of social and economic power in general. There is a corresponding glamourization of women's social and sexual subordination to men. The tensions in the plot are invariably resolved by, or at least buried in, marriage, and not any marriage, but a rigidly structured one in which the woman gives up her social autonomy with gay abandon in the hope of obtaining the love, i.e. protection, of an essentially dangerous male. Sexual surrender is tied to economic and social surrender. The woman, romantic soul that she is, makes no demands other than marriage itself in the naive belief that her big, strong hero will love as well as fuck her. If pornography is the depiction of women as the willing slaves of men, and in general the eroticization of institutionalized forms of domination, then one can hardly think of anything more pornographic than a lifetime of formula romance.

THE CENSORSHIP DEBATE

The most prevalent feminist approach to porn does not begin with erotic representation in general. Rather, it begins with a discussion of how the state could best be used to suppress violent porn. It is not a coincidence that feminist lawyers are playing an important role in the porn debate. They are primarily concerned with legal reform, and their definitions of porn are devised primarily for legal purposes. This is a problem in the debate. Feminist artists for example tend to approach the porn question differently, emphasizing the need for non-sexist representations and oppositional art, and expressing skepticism about censorship solutions.[6] But lawyers, who carry a lot more weight in certain sections of the women's movement, consistently examine pornography as a legal problem. This legal perspective does not necessarily coincide with that of the "average" woman.

The biggest umbrella group of women's organizations in Canada, the National Action Committee on the Status of Women (NAC), drafted a definition of porn for the federal government's Fraser Commission on Prostitution and Pornography. It emphasizes that sexual explicitness is not a problem. The problem lies in the representation of "violence against women," and the "submission" and "debasement" of women portrayed in such a way as to condone this degradation. Like most other women's groups, NAC called for the creation of a new Criminal Code pornography offence that would replace the present obscenity provisions.

This NAC definition was first presented in early February 1984, at the Toronto hearings of the Fraser Commission. In mid-March, NAC held its annual convention, where the delegates from hundreds of women's groups ratified this anti-porn position. A couple of delegates spoke against the vague wording of the definition, pointing out that many people think lesbian sex is degrading and debasing, and thus the NAC resolution (in the unlikely event that it became law) could be used to harass sexual minorities whose cultural products were disagreeable to mainstream society, or for that matter to the mainstream women's movement.

So the wording was changed to exclude the words "submission" and "debasement." The final wording however is still very vague. Porn is defined as "material which seeks to stimulate the viewer or consumer by depiction of violence, including *but not limited to* the depiction of coercion or lack of consent of any human being." Now, sexual harassment is undoubtedly coercion, but the glorified descriptions of sexual harassment that are part and parcel of formula romances and *Cosmo* fiction will not likely come under the scrutiny of the morality squad. If the NAC definition became law, it is far more likely that the police and the courts would choose to prosecute depictions of "kinky" sex which in their eyes condoned coercion.

Coercion and consent in the sexual sphere are not as easy to measure as the NAC resolution would have us believe. Some women might, for example, think that no woman could possibly consent to the sexual act of anal penetration, and that any pictures of a woman being "sodomized" necessarily constitutes pornography.

Indeed, the legal approach to porn tends to confuse reality and representation. In the real world a sexual assault is always objectionable. But how is one to determine whether or not the rape scene in *Tess of the D'Ubervilles* should be banned because it condones coercion? It is not at all simple to "read" the message in a particular picture; and even texts are often ambiguous. There are some pornographic texts and films that clearly endorse violence against women as a sexual turn-on. But there are many, many more which are not so unequivocal.

There is no clear line between depictions of consensual sex, of seduction and of coercion. Even in real life people disagree as to whether a woman has been coerced against her will or not (think of rape trials), And when we discuss representation the problems multiply, because there is no longer one person who claims to be the victim and whose interpretation carries particular weight. Legal skills might help to sort out a rape case, but they are powerless to give an authoritative reading of a particular picture or text.

This is why I have concluded that the attempt to present a definition of porn that even sexist policemen cannot misinterpret is futile. Two feminists might agree intuitively on what is offensive, although even among feminists there are major differences. But even if we agreed on what is offensive, it would be impossible to translate our critique of a representation into unequivocal legal language and then to ensure that the courts do not use these laws (ostensibly set up to protect women) in their efforts to persecute sexual minorities or ban representations that offend "community standards."

The legal approach cannot encompass the important questions of production, consumption, and context. Obscenity laws erroneously assume that images and texts have objective meanings. A judge is supposed to determine whether or not a magazine is obscene, and a film censor makes decisions about cutting films, with only the most cursory reference to the context and to how the intended audience consumes the product. New pornography laws might try to emphasize context a little more, but it is in the nature of legal proceedings to see cultural products as distinct entities with an absolute meaning.

Thus, I think the attempts to draw up anti-pornography legislation are, from a feminist perspective, bound to fail. Seeking state protection is a last-resort strategy. Empowering women is preferred to any policies granting yet more powers to an already overzealous police and court system. Especially dangerous are those attempts of cultural policy to regulate the production and consumption of representations by calling on the state to exercise its powers. An equal-pay law cannot be used against women, since its meaning and purpose is quite unambiguous. But any laws regulating representation can and are being used to suppress marginal or oppositional art, rather than the multinationals of pornography. The Toronto police recently confiscated a feminist art exhibit displayed in a bookstore window and charged the artists with obscenity (even though the display did not include *any* representations of explicit sexual activity, or of any human bodies, for that matter). We cannot reasonably expect those same policemen to understand what is truly degrading to women.

Nevertheless, an anti-censorship position is not by any means a do-nothing position. On the contrary. Spending a lot of time trying to change the laws can distract us from the necessary task of thinking creatively about what we women can and should do to replace both pornography and other sexist representations by woman-positive cultural projects. Some examples of what women can do to simultaneously attack the sexism of mass-produced culture and *empower* the women engaged in the action are as follows:

— boycott businesses that make money on pornography, and inform the management of our decision
— complain to bookstore owners and other storekeepers, not just about the presence of pornographic magazines but also about the absence of feminist periodicals
— use the handy "this degrades women" stickers available in women's bookstores to record our opinion of billboards, ads in the public transit system, and store window displays
— paint creative graffiti over billboards
— refuse to sell offensive magazines or rent offensive videos

in stores that we work in, making sure we get support from our union or from local women's groups
— try to educate the public about our concerns, by writing articles and letters to the editor, speaking in classrooms, organizing pickets at appropriate events
— challenge the men we know who use pornography, and the men we work with who put pin-ups up in public areas. Enlist the support of women workers and supportive men in the attempt to have a working environment that is misogyny-free! One can point out that pornography pollutes the emotional environment just like smoke pollutes the physical environment

In conclusion, it is becoming increasingly clear that pornography cannot be tackled as an isolated issue. If the main problem with porn is that it eroticizes the male sexual domination of women and other forms of social domination, then the only real solution is to empower women and other oppressed groups so that we can begin to redefine what is erotic and what is not. This will involve not only boycotting sexist cultural products and denouncing images which glamourize women's subjection, but also helping to create alternative cultural forms. More generally, since we have shown that a great deal of pornography's impact on us is due not to the images and words themselves but to the social context of men's actual domination of women, then anything we do to empower women and increase their sense of dignity and autonomy will help to rob porn of its power to humiliate us.

If pornography is taken out of its total social and cultural context, it can easily become a bandwagon issue for politicians to use in their own vote-getting campaigns. Equal pay would cost a lot of money, but a pornography law is free, and the right-wing moralists would also like it.

However, the issue of pornography can be used more positively and creatively to empower women. In this chapter I have tried to suggest some avenues for doing this. I have indicated that we need to turn our attention to the difficult problem of how our sexuality is shaped by cultural products, and in particular, cultural products which claim to satisfy our sexual desires (e.g. formula romances) while in fact robbing us of autonomous desires. I have also pointed out that the eroticization of gender oppression by pornography is equally present in other cultural forms, and that this is part of a larger problem of the eroticization of social relations of domination, including racism and class domination.

Pornography cannot be adequately dealt with by isolating and attempting to ban it. For one thing, pornography is not just a male product concocted to satisfy natural male desires. As we have seen, it affects both men and women and is deeply embedded in both the cultural and social relations of our society. Furthermore, a thorough analysis of pornography reveals the unpleasant truth that our task as feminists cannot stop with getting men to change their sexist practices and their traditional approach to sex. On the contrary. Even as we try to educate and change male behaviour, we also have to be courageous enough to turn the spotlight on *female* sexuality, and on feminine ideas about sexuality and feminine patterns of sexual behaviour. And if pornography and all the problems it raises cannot be accurately described as purely male, much less can anyone claim that female desire and women's sexual ethics are islands of purity and simplicity in a sea of male corruption. This then leads us to the final two chapters of this book, which deal with "Desire" (primarily feminine desire) and with "Ethics" respectively.

◆

CHAPTER SIX

IMAGINING DESIRE

IT IS PERHAPS a testimony to Freud's influence that in our own day the word "desire" refers primarily to sexual desire, and only secondarily to other types of desire. Some people have quarrelled with this tendency to give a privileged position to sexual desire, and have argued that sometimes "a cigar is just a cigar," or a thirst for knowledge is exactly that and not a sublimated erotic desire. And feminists have shown that the reduction of women's efforts to enter the public sphere to the simplistic and phallocentric concept of "penis envy" is simply the expression of Freud's sexism.

Whether or not we find Freud convincing (and I have mixed feelings about this) it does seem to be true that most desire in our society appears to have a sexual basis or overtone. One can overhear women discussing a shopping expedition in unabashedly erotic terms. They speak about "indulging themselves" and about "loving" particular pieces of clothing, and often the conversation will consist of one woman voicing her Puritan reluctance to give herself pleasure while the other woman encourages her to go ahead and never mind the (monetary) consequences.

If at the individual level there seem to be grounds for understanding sexual libido as the force fuelling all other desires, so too at the social level is there a parallel phenomenon. In Western capitalist societies since the eighteenth century there has been a tendency to equate sexual health with general social health, with "culture" and "civilization," while sexual "degeneracy" has been equated with the decline of empires and the breakdown of civilization.

All through the seventeenth and eighteenth centuries, educated European men (and a handful of women) devoured accounts of the bizarre sexual practices of the "savages" in Africa,

Asia and America. As Norbert Elias has pointed out in his insightful book *The History of Manners*[1], the discovery of "barbarism" was an essential element in the struggle of Europeans to define themselves as civilized. Some of these accounts stressed the inherent innocence and goodness of the "savages," and in that sense acted as a critique of European society. But many other accounts stressed the inherent barbarism of the savages and recounted in vivid detail the dreadful tortures undergone by white missionaries and other captives. In the nineteenth and twentieth centuries these semi-mythical accounts were instrumental in the institutionalizing of racism, for example in the process of wiping out most of the American Indian population.

Tales of interracial rape, ritual sodomy, and habitual polygamy were not only instrumental in the legitimizing of racist practices. They also acted to create a powerful image of the kind of sexual degeneracy that, it was feared, might crop up even among Europeans if the social control of desire was relaxed too much. Western civilization was allegedly based on the rise of the middle-class monogamous nuclear family in which sexuality, especially that of women and children, was tightly controlled to the point of suppression. Any challenges to the sexual norm were thus regarded as challenges to what was and still is grandiosely called "civilization."

If North American pioneer society lived in perpetual fear of the barbarians at the gates (with the understanding that the first thing the barbarians would do is have their way with "our" women), twentieth century "civilized" society fears the barbarian lurking in the heart of each one of us. Freud exposed one of the worst fears of his society when he pointed out that all children were inherently "polymorphously perverse," that is to say, had the capacity to eroticize any person or even thing. Freud also spoke of oral and anal eroticism as the basic forms of eroticism. Heterosexual intercourse might indeed be "natural," but it was not easy to grow into it.

In the societies that we call developed and civilized there exists, then, a constant anxiety about reverting to barbarism, and a constant fascination with those individuals or groups who are perceived to exemplify this degeneracy. Popular magazines like *The National Enquirer* are full of accounts of horrible crimes (if they are sexual crimes, so much the better) and of stories that crack the thin veneer of civilization. Babies with two heads; gay orgies; women who murder their husbands; husbands who keep their wives locked up in a box or a closet for years. This is the standard fare that feeds the audience's fascination with the degeneration of our society.

The highbrow equivalent to this is found in murder mysteries, which are based on the premise that the most genteel-looking English parson's wife could in fact be the grisly murderer who knifed seven people to death. Gothic romances are also based on the assumption that one's husband could turn out to be a Bluebeard clone, as Joanna Russ wittily argued in her essay "Somebody is trying to kill me and I think it may be my husband: the Modern Gothic".[2] "Evil lurks in the hearts of men" is one of those clichés which tell us a lot not about men or hearts but about the society which accepts it as truth.

It is my contention, then, that as a culture we are simultaneously repelled and fascinated by stories of "degeneracy" and most particularly of sexual degeneracy. And as we read about the doings of cocaine addicts in Hollywood or about the sexual perversities of a particular bizarre sect, our own sexuality is not totally free from scrutiny. We may shake our heads at stories about a fake guru who uses his charisma to entice young women into all kinds of sexual acts. But surely part of the appeal of these stories is that they always involve "normal" people, people like us, if only as victims of the evil initiator.

When we turn out attention away from the evil lurking in the hearts of others and reflect on our own passions, the same myths and fears about the fragility of civilization remain with us. We are not too sure that the socialization process has really worked. We are doubtful of our own ability to hold onto the values of "civilization" if we were to be put in an alien context and we wonder if we too could find ourselves in the pages of *The National Enquirer* as participants in a bizarre sex crime. It is this fear which is behind what I am calling here "the domino theory" of the passions: the fear that if we indulge in one prohibited passion, this will act as a domino toppling all other prohibitions.

THE "DOMINO THEORY"
OF THE PASSIONS

According to this view, which is really a myth having little basis in reality and a great deal of basis in paranoias and anxieties, passion and desire are dark forces, and civilization is a constant struggle to put external limits on them. Since, as Freud pointed out, sexuality is the least socialized of our passions, it plays a crucial role in this struggle. For essential to the myth is the view that the sexual passions have no self-regulating mechanism, no internal limits. Nobody worries about a philosopher indulging excessively in the desire for truth, but the "lower" passions as they are called are seen to have no internally produced limits. If left to themselves they would engulf everything in their path, reducing the individual to an irrational blob of lust and turning society into an increasingly violent orgy. (A good, non-sexual example of this is found in William Golding's novel *Lord of the Flies*, which posits just such a descent into raw passion and violence. It is curious that a story portraying English schoolboys engaged in playing out typically English and male ideas of what freedom from social constraint might look like is often interpreted as revealing profound insights into human nature itself.) Therefore, the lower passions are like "creeping communism": you give them an inch and they'll take a mile. If society grants permission for one taboo to be broken, then the passions will demand that yet another taboo be taken off the list, thus running roughshod over all decency and order.

This typically Christian view of passion is accepted both by the ideologues who produce pornography and by the moral conservatives who abhor it. The pornographers see the one-way, relentless growth of passion as just fine, or at least as natural, while moral conservatives and many feminists see it as a fundamental evil. However, both sides leave the basic model unquestioned.

A myth that is related to the domino theory could be called "the slippery slope." According to this myth, the one-way, limitless growth of sexual passion is by necessity a *downward* movement, an irreversible sinking into increasingly more perverse and more bizarre passions. The myth tells us that if you act on homosexual desires, then you will gradually degenerate into pederasty and child abuse. (This is only a sexual version of the old Puritan belief that one glass of wine inevitably leads to alcoholism, promiscuity, and syphilis.) The combined effect of the two myths is to ideologically organize sexual pleasures/desires along a downward spiral descending to absolute perdition. The particular desire perceived to be the first step to perdition is different for each person. For some, it's alcohol, for others drugs, and for many others a particular variety of sexual pleasure. So we often argue with one another about "where to draw the line" on desire, without ever questioning our basic framework of the spiral-shaped continuum.

These two myths underlie the fears expressed by many women about sexual experimentation. They also underlie the concerns voiced by anti-porn feminists about any attempt to reclaim sexual passions traditionally associated with the more degenerate male. There is a fear that if we reclaim the relatively innocent pleasure of the erotic gaze we will inexorably move on to actual erotic aggressiveness and from there to sadistic violence. We do not consider the possibility that some of the desires on the other side of the famous "line" might indeed turn out to be quite harmless or even life-affirming. Rather, they are all tainted by the brush of perversion and corruption.

Our social institutions confirm our worst fears about the cancerous growth of the passions. Society puts married couples in nice bungalows, and confines the seekers of one-night stands to seedy bars, thus creating the impression that the desire for erotic novelty is itself seedy. Another example: a woman going into a lesbian bar for the first time is not likely to reflect on the socio-economic basis of the lesbian bar's relative seediness. She is more likely to think, "Oh dear, is 'it' *really* like this?" as though the bar were a direct embodiment of lesbian desire itself. The unfortunate irony is that if certain groups are forced into dark and ugly corners of urban society, they are more likely to act in ways which match the decor of their particular ghetto.

Since by this time I have probably made most readers very uncomfortable, I want to address the objections that have accumulated in the reader's mind during the last few pages. Am I saying that *all* our fears of degeneracy and the loss of ethical and social values are completely unfounded? Am I saying I would refuse to "draw the line" at all and would allow all desires to flourish unimpeded? Do I have no morals? Do I not agree there are some people who do in fact threaten our social order and whose desires cannot be left unchecked?

My answer is that it is true that sexual desire sometimes takes misogynist, anti-social and cruel forms. I am not denying that some men are aroused by either degrading other people or seeing them degraded, and I would not regard this type of desire as a legitimate form of erotic desire. (For one thing, it frustrates the dialectic of mutual recognition which, as I argued in chapter one, is essential to eroticism.) But my point is that we will not be able to calmly address these ethical issues, which I attempt to discuss in the last chapter, unless we first do some ideological housecleaning and throw out some notions which we have used to sort good from bad but which are in fact quite irrational and unjustifiable. I will argue later that it is consumerism which constructs our desire as limitless, as infinite; neither human nature nor erotic desire should be blamed for the distortions of desire caused by such historical circumstances as consumerism and misogyny. So I am not saying that we do not in fact truly and honestly experience our passions as limitless, dark, and potentially destructive. But this experience is historically constructed. An analogy: in the Victorian period many women claimed to feel no active sexual desire at all. But was that not because they had internalized their society's values? Another analogy: in the days before gay liberation, many if not all homosexuals truly experienced themselves as abnormal, as not-women or not-men, as freaks of nature. I am arguing that our feelings about the dangers of sexual desire are as historically relative as the feelings of the Victorian ladies about heterosexual sex or the feelings of the nineteenth-century homosexual about same-gender sex.

The question is thus not so much whether the phenomena I have analyzed here are mere myths or are true reflections of our experience. Any myth worth its salt both reflects and shapes the collective experience of a particular culture. That is what makes it a myth and not a mere story that someone invents. Instead the question is, where did these myths come from and how did they lodge themselves in our psyches?

We have already suggested that the domino theory is of Christian origin. But similar theories are espoused in non-Christian societies as well. Other cultures and religions also set up intricate taboo systems, and classify passions according to a pre-established grid. What is perhaps particularly Christian is the "slippery slope" myth, the assumption that there is in every human being an inborn sinfulness, an inherent tendency to slide down the slope unless held in check by such external constraints as priestly authority, legal punishment, fear of hell, and last but not least, fear of social stigma. It is this idea which lends a quality of desperation to much of Christian moral theory, as compared, for instance, to the more creative and more confident moral systems developed by the ancient Greeks and Romans.[3]

But what about the domino theory as embodied in secular culture? Again, the little I know about non-Christian and non-bourgeois theories of passion suggests that our society holds to a particularly extreme version of a model which in different guises is operative in other cultures. Aristotle, for instance, thought there was indeed a need to classify, regulate and educate the passions; but for him the ethical ideal involved not blocking the passions but rather letting them develop within the limits set internally by each desire or need. That is, he believed that passions tended to generate their own natural limits. One did not have to fight tooth and nail against the growth of the passions, but only against the "artificial" growth that went beyond the boundaries set by the very nature of that particular passion. Factors such as timing and context were considered crucial in determining whether or not a passion developed naturally or unnaturally. His was not an abstract morality with absolutist rules. Now, the idea that passions have a natural limit is not any more "correct" than our own model, and is ideological in its own way (for instance, Aristotle assumed men and women had different natures and hence different proper passions). But it expresses a different set of values and beliefs than those of our own time, and thus provides a useful comparison.

The point is that Aristotle did not live in a consumer society. Consumerism has to actively reject any sense of a natural limit to need and desire so as to allow for increasing levels of consumption of increasingly more bizarre commodities. We are constantly being told that there is no such thing as enough money, enough pleasure, or enough power. We are told that the only limits to our desire to consume are set externally by the availability of money.

That sexuality has come to be understood and even experienced as a form of consumption, and thus subject to the relentless logic of the domino theory, is an unfortunate but understandable circumstance. In previous centuries, certain kinds of sexual activity might be seen as a kind of consumption (prostitution being the most obvious example), but sex within marriage was not necessarily interpreted from that point of view. In the twentieth century there has been a spectacularly successful attempt to bring the marketplace approach to sex into the home. Through the proliferation of sex manuals and other oracles of "exciting" heterosexuality, the task has been set for married couples: diversify your desires and maximize your pleasure. It is not sufficient to have sex, or even to have lots of sex. We have to "work at," as we say, "our sexual relationship" as though it were a family business. Pleasure is described in phrases taken out of stock-market reports, and desires are seen as analogous to investment possibilities. One problem that often arises when people try to live up to this is that the male and the female do not necessarily want to expand their pleasure business in the same directions. But the sex manuals ignore this conflict and glibly go on about how "you two" can experience "mutuality" and joint pleasure by increasing the number of sexual acts in your repertoire.

A gastronomic analogy might be useful to illustrate the problem of seeing sex, and desire in general, from the point of view of consumption. Most women in our culture, bombarded as they are by contradictory messages telling them both to be ridiculously thin *and* to enjoy all the artificial products of the food industry, have gotten hopelessly confused about their desires for food and the limits of their hunger. They live by the calorie book and have an irrational though not groundless fear that if they throw that book out the window, they will sink inexorably into a pig-like lifestyle. They honestly feel that if they cease to exercise a tight control on their appetite they will swell to the size of a car within weeks. My own anorexia was dominated by this irrational fear of my own desires, and even today I am not totally free of the paranoia that sees all absence of external constraint as a descent into primeval chaos. It is of course true that if one has dieted for a long time, going off the diet might lead to eating too much of the forbidden foods—for a time. But it is a complete myth that left to ourselves we would just go on and on eating. It is precisely the diet that causes the obsession with food and eating.

This does not mean, however, that there are such things as "natural" desires when it comes to food. Once I have listened to my own body enough to know when I am truly hungry, I go and choose how to concretize that general craving into a particular desire. And there the culture takes over. My desire for raw spinach would seem perverse in China; my pleasure in eating eggs fried in olive oil is definitely rooted in my Spanish childhood. It is important not to moralize about these desires. We could, however, try to eroticize (so to speak) foods which are in fact healthier, not for any moral reasons but for completely practical reasons.

Unfortunately, pragmatism is as difficult to implement in our gastronomic as in our sexual universe. Because of the myths described above, we are often unable to see past our own fears of irrevocable perdition. We therefore oscillate between guilt on the one hand and unbridled desires for the forbidden on the other. Apparently ordinary things like hunger and body size are perceived not as physical facts moulded by culture but as monsters who lurk in the hearts of women and men and are responsible for what we perceive to be our quintessentially human tendency to grossness and immorality. The demystification of passion and desire is thus not only a theoretically important project. It is also a matter of immediate and personal concern, involving our emotional and physical well-being as well as our erotic health.

THE SHAPING OF FEMALE DESIRE

Psychoanalysis envisions all sensual desires as based on the absence or lack felt by the baby when separated from its mother or from other sources of pleasure and nourishment.

This means that whatever the character of our desired objects, the form of our desire is often a longing not just to be with but to become one with the desired object. This longing is surrounded by a constant anxiety about loss, as both our actual separation from the mother, and our potential separations from other objects of desire.[4]

The male baby grows up to be a man whose masculine, phallic desires for the mother can then be satisfied to some extent by his conquest of women and of the world at large. The female, on the other hand, soon finds that the actualization of infantile desires is frustrated by the strong encouragement to redirect her energy and longing away from the maternal breast, in order to exclusively eroticize the male body. The original object of her desire, then, has to be completely repressed. Even if she accomplishes this redirection, and is comfortable in the heterosexual role, she will as an adult have particular, feminine difficulties in fulfilling her sensual desires. Her lack of power in the patriarchal world is one obvious problem. Another is that she not only has to change the nature of the desired object, but also the form of the desire itself. The baby's desires are enormous, selfish, and often destructive. They are shaped by the yearning to encompass everything, to absorb all alien or even potentially independent objects such as the breast into oneself. In adult life, men are allowed some measure of selfish desire, and as long as they do not exceed certain culturally determined boundaries they are rewarded and respected for showing ambition, drive, and ownership, in other words their mastery and power over other people and objects.

Women, on the other hand, are conditioned from a very early age to become mothers. Their desire is channelled into selflessness. Although Freud believes that there are unchangeable psychological reasons for women to transform their active, phallic desires into the desire to nurture a (male) child, the reasons for this transformation/distortion of female desire lie rather in the social structures of male dominated societies. In Freud's account, the bare physical fact of women's lack of a penis is used, by an interesting sleight-of-hand, to argue that women necessarily wish not only for a baby but for a whole nuclear family. From earliest girlhood our wish to possess and swallow up the Other is turned back, so to speak, and transformed into the opposite wish to be possessed by a stronger male. This is accompanied by the equally "innate" wish to become not just a biological but a social mother.

The complexities of human desire are thus simplified for us: women are offered only two basic forms of desire as possible models. One is the wish to become the object of male desire, giving up our autonomy to a stronger (male) will. The other is an identification with the "higher," selfless ideals of nurturing and mothering.

These two forms are actually two slightly different aspects of the same basic desire, as we see in the model of female desire provided by the image of the Virgin Mary. Mary bows before the (male) angel of the (male) Lord and says, "Thy will be done"; "I am the handmaiden of the Lord." She renounces all personal desires and instead embraces a mission to devote herself to a specific male (Jesus) and, through him, to the abstract values ordained by God. Her desire is to be the vehicle for God the Father's grandiose male desire to become flesh and dwell upon Earth. She is needed for this and can do it, because although she is basically flesh her "base" nature can be put to a "higher" use by giving birth to that peculiar combination of spirit and matter which is Jesus Christ. Men might get closer to God by chastity and bodily denial, but women, whose access to the realm of the spirit is in any case questionable because of their weaker intellect, can achieve a peculiarly feminine holiness by immersing themselves in their own flesh. Mary gets much closer to God than any other female saint precisely because she does not deny her "nature," her female body, but rather embraces it and puts it at the service of the Male Spirit.

If the Virgin Mary provides one powerful model of female desire, the apparent opposite model of Eve or the fallen woman turns out to be not so different. Eve has not succeeded in completely repressing her infantile desire for limitless power. The autonomous desire expressed in her wish to eat the fruit of the Tree of Knowledge symbolizes the ever-present possibility that women will refuse to be instruments of the Lord's will. Yet even the independence glimpsed in the Garden of Eden story is not real independence. Eve rejects the true Lord only when seduced by another male, the Devil. She would not have thought of eating the apple unless the serpent had offered it to her. So her rebellion against her role as instrument of God's will is firmly inscribed in the larger context of a power struggle between the two powerful male forces of God and the Devil. The difference between Eve and Mary may appear to be that between rebellion and submission. But on closer inspection the difference is rather between a Bad and a Good Master.

The secular equivalent of Eve is the whore. She too appears to transgress the female role because she actively "promotes lust" (the infamous words of an Ontario judge whose aim was to minimize the rape of a stripper). She often takes the initiative, and whether moved by her own lust or by the desire for financial gain she approaches men without waiting for them to make the first move. But again her seemingly active desires are released only after having been firmly tied to the larger context of patriarchal desire. She takes the lead, but her ultimate wish is to be dominated, overwhelmed, fucked. The ultimate whore, the "nymphomaniac" of male fantasies, is a woman who can't get fucked enough and whose unusually strong desires are still basically passive. She is therefore fulfilled when she finds a man who is strong enough to subdue her.

The content of the fallen woman's desire is different from the Madonna's, but the form is the same. Women mobilize a vast reservoir of psychological and physical energy in the service of male desire. Whether serving as vehicles for male goodness or for male evil, for salvation or for damnation, for spirit or for lust, women are never allowed to question the fact that they are essentially just vehicles. Women's purpose is to actualize goals or ideals or desires that did not originate with them. In this sense it is correct to say with Freud that female desire is the "dark continent," the great unknown of Western culture. It is not that we have not been allowed to have desires, but rather that we have not been allowed to express desires independently of male desire.

Since female desire is always relative, we need to examine how phallic desire is itself constructed. Before we turn our attention to phallic desire, though, it might first be useful to give some further examples of how women's desire is subordinated to masculine desire and shaped so as to reinforce the social structures of consumer, patriarchal capitalism.

Example 1

"Side dishes for four: Savoury Bean Salads. These luscious legumes, tossed with other zesty ingredients and served on sassy greens, are perfect for parties and picnics. From left: lentils in tangy, mustard-spiked dressing; crunchy three-bean combo. Snappy!"

This text is the introduction to a two-page *Cosmopolitan* magazine photo spread featuring the lowly bean "redeemed" by "zesty ingredients" and "sassy greens" and presented in a fairy-tale, make-believe context of splendour, class, and sensual pleasure. Recipes are of course included, but the emphasis is on the overall sensual experience, not the details of how this can be produced, or rather reproduced, by the female reader.

This feature is meant to appeal simultaneously to several female desires. Some of these are rooted in such natural wants as the need to eat, but most desires implicated and created by the magazine feature are unabashedly social and even artificial. Let us look at them in some detail, grouping them into a few categories.

FOOD

Our natural hunger is stimulated by the glossy photos portraying larger than life lentils and beans (not the most appetizing of foods!) looking "luscious" indeed (lighting effects) and even "zesty" (colour scheme created by adding parsley, onions and carrots). Our tastebuds are also stimulated by the words themselves: "sassy," "tangy," "crunchy," "zesty." And our tastebuds seem to be, judging by the words used, peculiarly feminine. The word "crunchy" has child-like connotations, with breakfast cereals being the crunchy food par excellence in the symbolic universe of advertising. "Sassy," "tangy," and "zesty," especially used together, are hopelessly feminine words. As further proof of femininity, there is here no meat or any other food primarily associated with men. However, once the woman's feminine tastebuds have been stimulated, she is not allowed to seek satisfaction by eating the food herself. The quantity of the food is specified—for four—and we all understand without having to be told that the word "four," especially when accompanied by a picture of wineglasses, means two men and two women, and more specifically two couples. So from what appears to be a factual element of a recipe we derive social prescriptions about heterosexuality and about constituting ourselves as a couple.

SEX

Beans and lentils are not exactly glamorous or romantic foods. Even they, however, can be rescued from the lowly task of feeding the body and put to the "higher" purpose of promoting sexual interaction. For they are drenched in "tangy" (read sexy), "mustard-spiked dressing." As if that weren't enough, we are specifically instructed to produce these dishes for "parties and picnics." Say no more! The "luscious legumes" idealized in the photo look like they are about to gratify, in an immediate and satisfying way, our desire for food and for the reaffirmation of the heterosexual couple. This pleasure must be delayed, however. Bean salads do not appear out of nowhere, and they cannot be bought at a deli, as a man would do if faced with the challenge of getting provisions for a picnic. No, they have to be produced, and it is understood they will be produced by a woman in her own home. She will use up her time shopping, arranging, chopping onions, measuring oil and vinegar, soaking the beans, cooking, opening cans and cleaning up. A certain number of skills are involved, from knowing how to crush garlic to having an eye for visual presentation. All this work is supposed to be undertaken by virtue of our sex, because this is what women do.

Although the photos and recipes stimulate the woman's own appetite and not that of her potential guests, the food is supposed to be produced for the exclusive pleasure of the already constituted couples. A survey of women's magazines reveals few recipes designed for the pleasure of the single woman; they live on diets. Pleasure in eating is only allowed when one cooks *for* men and eats *with* men. Thus, our impulse to eat and our desire to eat well are subordinated to the needs of the larger social world. We women get to eat well only as a side effect of preparing a good meal for the family or for the men in our lives. When alone or with other women we are supposed to deny ourselves pleasure and stick to salads and Perrier. The steady diet of lettuce and diet Coke, however, gets so oppressive that we sometimes go out with the girls and "pig out," almost invariably on sweets. But the consumption of desserts is not an unmitigated pleasure, surrounded as it is by caloric guilt and quasi-moral anxieties about gaining weight.[5] It is as though eating well without men's company were akin to masturbating—a base pleasure to be repressed and harnessed to the institution of heterosexuality and the family.

CLASS

Again, beans and lentils are hardly upper-class kinds of food. Recipes for lobster or for champagne-drenched desserts have an obvious class bias; whereas one would think a lentil salad would be the sort of thing a woman on welfare could afford. However, poverty is a taboo in women's magazines. One can be "on a budget," which is a euphemism for poverty, but God forbid that any of the efficient and glamorous readers of magazine X should actually be poor. Hence, the cheapness of the foods has to be disguised. This is done by various methods: pseudo-pornographic pictures that make yellow wax beans look like gold; recipes that call for red wine vinegar, Dijon mustard and olive oil.

The message appears to be: you may be a single woman without much money for lavish dinners at home, but you can maximize your meagre resources by giving beans and lentils a veneer of class. When your boyfriend says "What a nice dressing," you can respond "Isn't it nice, it's the Dijon mustard that makes it." And the boyfriend will think "The girl really has class . . . I wonder what she could do with steak."

The mouth-watering pictures and descriptions of bean salads are not really meant, then, to satisfy women's own desires for good food. Rather, they prey upon these desires in order to reinforce both patriarchal values (women cooking for men, compulsory heterosexuality, the subordination of women's pleasure to that of couple or family) and consumerist, middle-class values (the lowly lentil has to be disguised with exotic dressings and surrounded by expensive wine glasses). The bean salad feature *creates* certain desires in the women readers, desires which have as their main object a certain lifestyle essentially defined by class, gender, and sexual orientation. The lentil is like Cinderella: it has shed its obscure and spinsterly origins and has magically become the symbol of the comforts of middle-class heterosexual life.

For our next example, let us turn to the distortion/creation of specifically sexual desires.

Example 2

Question: My "problem" is that I much prefer foreplay and oral sex to intercourse. I don't see anything all that odd about these inclinations, but most of my lovers do. Should I seek help? I'm orgasmic during the kind of sex I like.

Answer. Preferring such activities isn't necessarily a problem, but the fact that you make men aware of your proclivities in a manner they find upsetting leads me to suspect you may have hostile feelings toward them . . . . Possibly, you shy away from penetration because you fear being hurt by closeness. While cunnilingus and other preliminary techniques can indeed be an important part of intimacy, these methods, used alone, also serve as a way of avoiding more personal contact . . . .

—"Analyst's Couch"
by William S. Appleton, M.D. Psychiatrist

Dr. Appleton, who has read Freud but not *The Hite Report*, is the *Cosmo* oracle on emotional health. Women who are otherwise enjoying themselves leading the liberated *Cosmo* lifestyle are encouraged to peer into their lives and discover a "problem" that Dr. Appleton can solve, much as Catholic children are supposed to construct sins out of their experience for the satisfaction of the priest's desire. The letter writer has discovered that she likes sex, and she enjoys it when men make love to her. (This is referred to by Dr. Appleton as "proclivities" and "preliminary techniques".) On the other hand, she doesn't much like intercourse, possibly because it hurts, or simply because it's boring. She has thus managed, despite her upbringing and despite hundreds of years of patriarchal attempts to deny women pleasure, to find her source of sexual pleasure and seek satisfaction. And yet, enough patriarchal attitudes have seeped into her mind that she wonders "Should I seek help?" even while adding that she does have orgasms.

The doctor, who would never wonder if *he* should seek help if his wife were less than ecstatic with their lovemaking, decides that she does indeed need help. Identifying completely with the male lover's frustrations, he knows enough not to attack the woman directly. So he doesn't just say "Male pleasure is what counts, you fool." No, that would give the game away. So he pretends that it's "natural" and "normal" to regard intercourse as the final goal of all sexual activity, thus reducing sex to sex for the man. If the woman avoids vaginal penetration, it can't be for the prosaic reason that she derives no pleasure from it, since woman's pleasure is not the purpose of sex as defined by Dr. Appleton. It must be—surprise!—because she is a cold, frigid bitch, despite all evidence to the contrary. She must be "hostile" to men, for any woman who puts her own pleasure ahead of men's must be pathologically anti-male. She "fears being hurt by closeness." The fact that many men actually hurt their female lovers when having intercourse is irrelevant. Women must surrender to the great penis in order to be true women, and their own pleasure or pain are indeed irrelevant.

The woman's desires are thus turned into pathological symptoms. Without actually saying so, Dr. Appleton suggests that women must be delighted to let male orgasms determine the shape and rhythm of lovemaking, leaving their own pleasures to the second class status of "foreplay" and "preliminaries." But her great sin does not lie in her actual sexual desires; the main problem is that she "upsets" men by revealing them. *Cosmo*'s Dr. Appleton is not a Victorian; he is vaguely aware that women have sexual pleasures of their own. But according to him women should silence their desires and simply try to manipulate the situation so as to maximize their own pleasure; they must never actually confront men.

This example reveals the fundamental contradiction of the *Cosmo* ideology, which proclaims women's right to have affairs and even be aggressive both in and out of bed—while never facing up to the fact that at some point both the boy-friends and the Dr. Appletons are going to find their authority directly challenged. *Cosmo* portrays women with glamorous jobs and even more glamorous lovers. But it never shows direct struggle between those women and the men in their lives. If things get out of hand, women are encouraged to dump their lovers. But during the affair the satisfaction of women's own desires must always be carefully orchestrated so that women's pleasure does not threaten the basic structure of the relationship. Women are encouraged for example, to spruce up their sex lives by fantasizing various taboo situations while making love. This is something they can do on their own, without any need to talk to men about their desire.

Female desire does exist, then, and indeed is constantly created and recreated by the culture in which we live. But female desire does not originate in women's autonomous existence. Neither is it rooted in a woman-positive community, a harmonious social whole whose requirements could be internalized by women without any need for the distortion or suppression of their desires. In our society, we enjoy neither individual freedom nor the benefits of a well-ordered collectivity. Our desires are constructed by the same forces that produce patriarchal structures and individual sexist men. Sometimes our desire is stimulated so that our energies can be channelled into satisfying men's pleasure (as Dr. Appleton advises). Other times, our desire is exploited for the benefit of the group (when women's hunger is "fed" by instructions on how to cook for their family). Modern sexual liberation theories threaten to undermine the old conceptual framework which reserves all desire for the male. So vast amounts of energy are being mobilized into making sure that women's new-found sexual freedom is orchestrated by and for men. The modern male lover "gives" his woman orgasms. That much is allowed since the superiority of the penis is left unchallenged. What is not allowed is for the woman to speak freely of her own desires, to name her pleasures directly and not as relative to the male's. We can accept men's "gift" of sexual desire—as long as we do not point out that it was not theirs to give in the first place. Women's desire has to be shaped so as to allow for an appearance of wildness, a veneer of autonomy. But its development, radical as it is in comparison to the ideal of passionlessness, still takes place within a phallocentric context.

THE NEW SPIRIT OF CHIC
MASCULINE DESIRE

If females are subject to a process which subordinates the naming and the realization of their desire to the development of masculine desire, then one might think male desire is somehow free from distortion, and that what we see out there (aggressiveness, competition, rape) is indeed the expression of man's "true" desires. Yet this conclusion is completely false, for it ignores the complicated process by which males are "gendered" or made masculine. From the time the kindergarten teacher says "boys don't cry" males are instructed in the behaviour and feelings appropriate to the claims of masculinity. Anxiety, sadness, confusion, weakness, affection and fear are some of the emotions that are supposed to be rooted out and replaced by a small selection of acceptable feelings: aggressiveness, competition, pride and courage.

This is not to say that masculinity is also an oppression, as some rather naive men have concluded. It is not an oppression because it is designed precisely in order to allow men to dominate women, and men of lower classes and races, in a "natural" way without self-reflection or guilt. The process of instilling masculinity in individual men does limit and stunt their growth. But these limitations are constructed so as to fit men into a structure which gives them privilege, power and wealth. Even men who are not at the top of the male pyramid by virtue of their class, colour or sexual orientation have power at least over some groups of women.

Most of the requirements of masculinity—especially in a capitalist society, where competitiveness and ruthlessness are economically rewarded—involve creating in men the kinds of desires which often result in violence. However, just as some of the desires created in women by the requirements of femininity are not in and of themselves negative (such as the desire to nurture), neither are all masculine desires completely dis-agreeable. The desire to work hard and to create a good product (as found in craftsmen, skilled male workers and male farmers) is a worthy one. But its expression may lead to deplorable consequences if it involves a ruthlessly individualistic climb to the top, or a collective assertion of superiority over "inferior" groups. The pride of white male skilled workers is often inter-twined with sexism and racism so it can often be associated with exclusivist union policies and other retrograde measures. For example, English male typesetters and printers have expe-rienced their skills as virtually synonymous with both their maleness and their Englishness, and to defend their skill against technology-caused deskilling is for them equivalent to defending the trade against women and Irish men. However, there is still a skill worth defending, even if the strategies chosen by the men in question are reactionary.[6]

This example points to a larger problem in the understand-ing of masculine desire. Because all desire has been concep-tualized and experienced as primarily masculine, it is difficult to sort out which aspects of masculine desire are rooted in patriarchal domination, and which have been appropriated by masculinity but belong to the human species at large.

Moving from the working world to the world of aesthetic and erotic pleasure, we can ask: is the desire to look at pictures which are both aesthetically and erotically pleasing a specifically male desire? Or is it, like the desire to realize oneself in skilled work, one which has been inextricably linked to gender and race privilege but which one could imagine as being separate from the system of domination?

Some people believe it is only men who enjoy looking at pictures of naked bodies, and that this desire is rooted in male-ness. Women might have an intellectual appreciation of high art but, so the argument goes, even the classic masterpieces are essentially male, with females being portrayed as objects or static symbols. Women therefore cannot really enjoy art or films or sculpture, because in order to do so they would have to identify with the male point of view of the artist or camera. Even if they can momentarily take this position, they constantly fall back into an identification with the object, thus prevent-ing their visual erotic pleasure from being realized.[7]

There is a lot of truth in this argument. Analysis of the "system of looks" governing both painting and film conventions reveals that the male gaze is always the authoritative one, while the female gaze only responds or answers. (In Hollywood films, the points of view of the main male character, camera, and spectator tend to be collapsed into one. We don't just look at a man looking at a woman, we *are* the man looking at the woman.) Yet it is not clear whether the very pleasure of looking is hopelessly mired in masculine power, or whether it could be rescued, so to speak, and used to affirm women's desire and pleasure. This cannot be done by a simple inversion of the system of looks: a man being stared at by a woman would seem and feel himself to be ridiculous, not erotic at all. We would tend to avert our eyes and not identify with that female gaze. Similarly, a painting depicting a standing, fully clothed woman looking down at a reclining, wan male nude would also provoke giggles, not aesthetic admiration. The reasons for this are complex, but they have to do with the fact that inversions of gender roles are at the heart of what we consider to be comic or ridiculous, and the comic is incompatible with the erotic (as mentioned in chapter one).

So we cannot just trade places in the pictures, for how we experience those pictures is necessarily determined by the social reality in which we live. In a world where women were powerful, the female gaze would connote authority, active desire, and truth. But in our world this is not so, and we cannot arbitrarily change the meaning of well-established symbols.

Yet once in a while we can get a glimpse of what it's like to have a gaze that can convey both authority and desire without implicating ourselves in masculinity. The work of some women artists sometimes depicts "classic" female nudes that manage not to be classic at all because instead of turning the model into an object they seem somehow to endow it with the same power that the woman obviously has in real life. I have a drawing in my living room of a classic nude woman. Drawn by a lesbian, the figure begins at the chin and stops just above the crotch: there is no face to give the body expression and individuality and rescue it from the objectified status of the "classic nude." Yet, a very strong and active hand, shown in the foreground and drawn with bold, dark strokes, accomplishes the purpose. The body is beautiful in a traditional sort of way, and probably looks "passive" just because it's a woman's body with bare breasts. However, the arm and hand suggest power, individuality—a desire that is autonomous and not merely a response to the viewer's desire.

When I look at the drawing I experience the kind of aesthetic pleasure I can also get from looking at Henry Moore's sculptures or Picasso's drawings. At the same time I experience a very different kind of pleasure, one that is more specifically erotic. I do not just see an object; I see an object which is also a subject and which, though unknown to me, clearly has a life of her own.

When the viewer's gaze is defined in conventional ways, it is associated with masculinity and with one-way power. But if we change the context and the connotations of power, we can have a situation in which there is still a one-way gaze (I look at the drawing of a woman who has never looked at me), but the form of the visual/erotic desire is different. Although some feminists hold that all representations of female bodies are per se objectifying and sexist, I think there are instances, however exceptional, which prove that the connection between visual/erotic pleasure and masculinity is not a necessary one and can be broken. The desire to gaze, even to gaze at naked female bodies, *could* be rescued. (I say "could" because I feel uneasy when male visitors look at my drawing, and my uneasiness is well-founded.) If men did not in reality have so much power over women, the male gaze would not objectify everything it touches.

Even in today's world however men do not always make use of the stereotypically male gaze to look at women. For instance, when I am at the gym there are plenty of semi-nude female bodies to be seen. But because they are not on display but are rather actively sweating, and because the men are also occupied in strenuous activity hardly suitable for a voyeur, the men's looks are rarely objectifying or degrading. They probably know that any woman there could easily fix them with a good long stare at their all-too visible sexual equipment. They thus steal surreptitious admiring looks but do not engage in an unambiguous voyeurism that could so easily be turned back on them. And I for one (heretical as this might sound) do not equate their surreptitious admiring looks with sexist objectification, especially when the woman who is the object of the look is in the midst of an activity demonstrating her strength and endurance. Such a look may be partially objectifying; but it also acknowledges the power and desire of the Other.

Nevertheless, masculine eroticism tends to be marked by ownership, aggressiveness, and a lack of acknowledgment of the other person's desires. As stated at the beginning of this section, masculinity may limit men and prevent them from certain kinds of emotional growth, but these constraints are there for men's own good, so to speak. Thus, feminists should not expect that men will be as keen to divorce themselves from masculinity as we are to shed the humiliating aspects of femininity.

Indeed, I know no instances of heterosexual men willingly relinquishing their masculine habits and privileges, except when this process was pushed along by either a female partner of independent ideas or by the collective weight of the women's movement (and usually a combination of both). Although men and women can be described as equally handicapped in their erotic life, women's handicaps, based on the subordination of their desires, are more clearly problematic. Men's handicaps, while they may result in impoverished emotional lives, are associated with a great deal of social and sexual power. To recognize the limits of masculine eroticism is to challenge the very real privileges men have in the actualization of their desire. The *Cathy* cartoon strip summarized the situation: "Men say they are oppressed because they can't cry— but they never had anything to cry about."

It would thus be naive to expect men to spontaneously give up their masculine dominance. Such a move might, in the long run, result in more fulfilling lives, but in the short run a lot of losses and insecurities are involved. Besides, men get a lot of peer pressure not to be or appear to be "hen-pecked." Heterosexual women will thus have to continue to push the men they love, despite the problems these struggles entail. It is possible, though, that there may be more men willing to enter into such a struggle, not just for the love of a particular woman, but out of a sense of justice and long-term change.

AGGRESSIVENESS AND PASSIVITY

One of the themes of this book is the need for women to name and claim desire in all its complexity, without making a priori judgements about which, if any, aspects of desire are fundamentally male or female. We can decide this only once we have had access to all facets of desire.

This is why I want to undertake an analysis of erotic aggressiveness and passivity that does not involve naturalistic assumptions about gender roles, such as assuming that men are by nature erotically aggressive. We must also steer clear of the domino theory's assumption that aggressiveness necessarily leads to sadism or that consensual sadomasochistic sex necessarily leads to violence. To assume this would be tantamount to accepting the police view of "perversion" ("They start with rock videos and move on to kiddie porn," "They start with pot and soon they're hooked on heroin"). Rather than rely on these images of perverted passion running amok, we would do well to listen to the contradictions within passion, and to the experiences that do not fit our preconceived models.

We can still leave open the possibility that biting your lover's nipple is the polite expression of hidden violence. Perhaps there is an inherent sadism in active desire, and a corresponding masochism in passive desire. But this is not necessarily true. If we want to argue that it is, we have to offer concrete proof, not just domino theories.

Let us now move on to an analysis of sadistic and masochistic desires. The first thing to do is clarify the different meanings which these much-mystified terms can have. Taking masochism as our main focus, since it has been traditionally associated with women, we can distinguish at least five different meanings for the concept or the word "masochism."

(1) Masochism can mean a desire to be erotically conquered or overwhelmed, to let someone else "have their way" with us: a particularly strong form of passive eroticism. This first

meaning of masochism is not masochistic at all, in the sense that it does not imply inferiority or self-contempt. It can be a *happy* feeling of wanting/expecting to receive the powerful erotic force of a lover.

(2) Some people would also include under masochism the erotic desire for sex that includes a certain degree of roughness (bites, sudden penetration, anal sex, etc.). Again, this is not necessarily a desire for pain itself. When sexually aroused one's sensitivity to pain greatly decreases, and "rough" sex, within certain limits, is experienced not as painful but as fulfilling. Acts that would in non-sexual circumstances or in coercive sexual experiences be certainly felt as painful are not always felt as such during willing sex. However, some people do seek out actual pain in the course of obtaining sexual pleasure. This might take place at the same time but is a distinct form of desire.

(3) What most people call masochism is the obtaining of sexual pleasure through the infliction of physical pain. I suspect this is not a major constituent element in many women's desire, but that it might at times be an element in the desires described in (1) and (2).

(4) Another meaning of the term masochism refers to the mostly non-sexual desire for humiliation and degradation. This is often linked to self-loathing and/or a generalized contempt for sex and the body. According to some psychologists, people with strict religious upbringings sometimes feel they have to be "punished" for their lust. By receiving sexual pleasure and degradation at the same time they can assuage both their sensual wants and the claims of their moralistic super-ego.

(5) Finally, some people practice a largely ritualistic, symbolic version of s/m that involves "props" (leather, garters and lace, uniforms of various sorts) and "scripts" (e.g. master/slave, teacher/pupil, cop/criminal). A substantial minority within both the gay male and the lesbian community practice this consensual s/m, and according to the participants, the "bottom" is always in control of the limits of the game. Sometimes

the game involves rough sex; sometimes it involves a certain amount of controlled violence, e.g. the person playing the cop putting handcuffs on the person playing the criminal and proceeding to rough up the "suspect." However neither one of these is necessary. Sometimes sex never actually takes place because the partners become absorbed in role-playing. According to some lesbians who both practice and preach this form of s/m, the main appeal of the game is not so much the physical acts but rather the "exchange of power" that takes place. Although the "top" has apparently absolute power over the other person's pain and pleasure, she/he has this power only insofar as the "bottom" confers trust on the top. Thus, the power is more equal and reciprocal than a casual observer would think.

I might add that much of the theory produced to justify ritual s/m has been produced by gay people, and it is difficult to see to what extent these justifications could apply to a heterosexual situation in which the woman is relegated to the position of slave/pupil/bottom. Given patriarchal prescriptions, it is hard to see how a woman could *freely* desire to totally give up her power to a man, when he already has so much power over her by virtue of being male. It might be possible, however, to disentangle personal desire from social compulsion enough to allow for such a possibility.

These five meanings of masochism which have five correlate meanings of sadism) must be kept distinct if we are going to understand the dialectic of aggressive/passive desire. I would tend to confine the term "masochism" to meanings (3) and (4), while reserving the term 's/m' for (5) and finding some other term for the desires described in (1) and (2).

Indeed, the desire described in (1) is just half the dialectic of erotic desire described in the first chapter. Thus, rather than seeing it as a form of "masochism"—a term which inevitably suggests something pathological, regardless of how neutral one tries to be—it is more accurate to see it in the context of reciprocal erotic power. Passive eroticism is but a moment, a facet, of eroticism, and even though women are socialized to stay frozen in that role I think most women would admit to harbouring the opposite, aggressive aspect of desire.

By describing aggressive and passive desires as two moments of a dialectic, I am not saying that all we need to do to overcome and transcend rigid roles and their gender connotations is merely to exchange places back and forth, "Now I'm active, you be passive, then we'll trade." The trade is of course important, since it gives the lie to the notion that some of us, primarily women, are essentially passive, while others, notably men, are essentially aggressive. But there is more to dialectics than simple exchange. What "dialectics" means is that each opposite contains the other. The interplay of the two opposites is found not only in the middle, in the air between two solid entities, but also in each of the two extremes.

A concrete example will help to illustrate this. If I am in the active role at one particular moment, for example seducing someone, an integral part of this active seduction is a strong, incredibly sweet feeling of giving in, giving up, willingly submitting to my lover's growing desire. I may be doing all the visible work, unbuttoning shirts and kissing and creating arousal; but my lover is not a mere object, and the response I see is not mechanical. My lover's response is desire itself, a desire which may express itself in primarily passive eroticism for a while, but which always has the potential to engulf me, throw me backwards, to overwhelm me. What I see and feel in the body of the lover is not weakness, but strength. This strength expresses itself in a primarily passive manner but is undoubtedly as powerful and potentially active as my own active strength. And when I go from seduction to lovemaking, even if I'm the one who is still superficially "doing the work" (not in any case an adequate description) I am not all aggressiveness while the other is all passivity. When I stimulate my lover I am fulfilling my own desire to be sexually aggressive. At the same time, I am *identifying* with her pleasure, both her physical response and her yearning to receive my erotic force. I do not just see her yearning out there but also feel it within myself. When making love to a man, a woman can't identify quite as thoroughly with the physical process he is engaged in; but she can still identify completely with his emotional arousal, his desire, pleasure and fulfilment.

Clearly, this interplay of complementary desires that define themselves both by opposition and identification cannot be adequately described by the rather mechanistic phrase of "exchanging roles." It is not as if at one point I run backstage, shed one costume and put on another. Active and passive desire always contain each other, or at least the germ of each other. Even when only one role is played desire does not remain static and unambiguous. Erotic interchange is not a tennis game in which desire is a thing that gets thrown back and forth between two distinct participants. The movement *within* each player is the ground for the interchange that we observe *between* them.

Once we understand how active and passive desire constantly create each other as opposites and at the same time constantly merge into one another, we will be in a better position to make choices and decide if we indeed want to make changes in our eroticism. Perhaps we are reluctant to admit aggressiveness as being truly "ours," and so need to create safe situations in which to explore that aspect of ourselves. Perhaps we will find we are happy in limiting ourselves most of the time to one of the two roles. There is no law anywhere saying that lovers have to be active 50 percent of the time and passive the other 50 percent.

But even if we are primarily drawn to one of the two poles, we need to recognize that the other is also within us. If we fully identify with the desire of our lover, then that means we have the potential to feel and act on that desire too. We may choose to be unconventional, to use sex toys or play games involving roles and scripts. But the toys and the games are not much fun if used to disguise the movement of desire and fix people in certain roles like figures in a wax museum. The accoutrements of sexuality are best used to reveal the movement and the dialectic of desire, not to conceal or freeze it at a particular moment. And these accoutrements include both conventional rituals—romantic dinners and candlelight—and less conventional rituals like sex toys. I do not believe there are any inherently moral or immoral, better or worse, sexual rituals.

Some rituals, however, tend to reinforce the myth of "essential" roles for lovers of different genders, races, and social status. Some common s/m scenarios come to mind, like the cop/criminal or macho man/woman in high heels and lace.

The advocates of s/m often claim they are not necessarily "buying into" the social roles used in their sexual games, and that the roles are only fantasy or, as some have argued, that they actually ridicule those who live by them in real life. There is a grain of truth to these arguments, but on the whole I think they overestimate the power of individuals to determine at will the social meaning of certain signifiers and roles. The reason s/m relies so heavily on highly unequal and stereotyped roles is precisely because these roles have a tremendous power which can be used to fuel erotic exchanges. This power is not present in other possible erotic scripts such as two androgynous people seducing each other. Whether their intent is to use erotic scripts to reinforce social relations of domination, or whether they simply see them as fantasies without much connection to real life, the fact remains that they are using forms of power which a sexist and exploitative society has produced. It may be possible to use these forms in order to defuse or undermine their social meaning, but one would have to be constantly struggling to prevent oneself from sinking comfortably into the "usual" dynamics of power and the "normal" meanings of the roles and images being used.

However, I grant the advocates of consensual s/m their point that at least they are aware of the role-playing involved. Two people involved in an erotic game in which one of them gets dressed up as a cop know that nobody is born with the power of a policeman, and that this power is conferred on individuals by certain social forces embodied in certain symbols.

By contrast, "normal" couples who are permanently stuck in unequal roles see them not as socially constructed, but as natural forms of behaviour. They might firmly believe that Nature decrees that the man should be on top of the woman during sex, or that women should let their male lovers and friends pay for their dinners. These roles are thus more nefarious because they are unconsciously assumed, even if the behaviour involved is fairly innocuous and less remarkable than the exotic antics of those who enjoy making love wearing black leather jackets and studded collars.

We began this chapter by criticizing some concepts of passion and desire which carry a great deal of weight both in our culture and in our individual psyches, and which actively prevent us from both thinking clearly about and experimenting with our desires. These mythic fears, which we labelled "the domino theory" and the "slippery slope", are supplemented and reinforced by the numerous injunctions originating in patriarchally constructed models of masculinity and femininity. Finally, we tried to examine how erotic aggressiveness and passivity work, rejecting both the myth that these two aspects of desire are sex-linked, and the even more prevalent myth that any desire can be frozen in time and separated from the dialectically opposite desire. We tried to avoid naturalism, and to be attentive to the ways in which desires both posit their opposites, and contain the germ of, and actually turn into, that opposite.

By destroying the myth of fixed, object-like desires, this approach enables us to see and understand not only the power of the social and cultural determinants of desire, but also the less visible but crucially important forms of resistance to those social forces. Feminist theory has done a lot to reveal the roots of some of the myths about desire, most notably the myth that women are by nature masochistic. But it has yet to deepen its analysis to include those myths which are not directly gender-based, such as the domino theory of passion. The analysis presented here is thus an attempt to move the discussion forward not only by offering a few new ideas but also by arguing for a new methodology suited both to the topic at hand (desire, which cannot be grasped statically) and to the unabashedly political aim of transforming desire itself by seizing the social and cultural forces which create and shape our innermost passions. Whether or not readers agree with the ideas and conclusions presented here, I hope they will at least try out the method. Nobody has the monopoly on either the experience or the theory of desire. All that writers can do is demystify and undermine myths and ideologies, and suggest ways of thinking about our experience which do not presuppose the social system that we are trying to critically analyze. But that is no small contribution.

♦

CHAPTER SEVEN

PLEASURE AND ETHICS

As FEMINISTS we face a number of difficulties when we begin to think about moral or ethical values. One of the first choices we have to make concerns the relative usefulness of "universal" (which means primarily masculine) values and laws, as opposed to "female" or "feminine" values.

Some contemporary feminist theorists, notably Carol Gilligan, have tried to reclaim "feminine" moral and intellectual qualities and use them to develop an ethical system congruent with women's experiences and aspirations. Since the suffrage movement at the turn of the century, feminists have pointed out that the existence of moral qualities which have been traditionally assigned to women (nurturance, empathy, selflessness) suggest the possibility that brute force and competition need not rule the world. Many early feminists thought that if these principles were to guide the public and not just the private sphere, then the world would be, in the words of Canadian suffragist Nellie McClung, "A sweeter, cleaner, safer place than it is now!"

Feminists have also pointed out that the positive aspects of "feminine" morality can be distinguished from the more negative characteristics of self-abasement and loss of self-worth. Furthermore, the fact that women are more sensitive and caring does not mean they are necessarily less rational than men. Carol Gilligan has argued[1] that women's "intuitive" empathy with others has been disparaged and dismissed as infra-rational by male ethical thought. But, Gilligan says, it is socially advantageous that women are able to see both sides of a moral dilemma and to engage in a moral reasoning that pays attention to concrete circumstances. Men, on the other hand, tend to make abstract judgements based on universal and inflexible rules. Gilligan suggests that by paying attention to the way women actually make moral decisions—by balancing conflicting interests and reflecting on the consequences of the decision for all parties involved—society as a whole might be able to begin to construct a more humane, less abstract and less sexist moral system.

Yet the problem with any attempt to rectify the sexist bias of traditional ethical and moral theory is that there is no such thing as a universal "women's experience" that we can point to and use as our basis to build a more useful and less judgemental moral system. Apart from gender-specific values, each culture and each social group within that culture have also certain general ideas about right and wrong, duties, and natural or unnatural acts, and these affect both men and women. These ideas or standards, which have usually had an ambiguous character, have been seen both as absolutely universal *and* as particularly suited to male ethical subjects.

An example of this, brilliantly examined by Adrienne Rich in *Women and Honor: Some Notes on Lying*, concerns the traditional requirement to be honourable and tell the truth.[2] This appears to apply to both sexes equally, yet women have traditionally been considered unable to clearly distinguish truth from falsehood. They have been viewed as naturally deceptive beings who are unaware of the importance of truthful language. The phrase "a man's word" means that a man is telling the truth and is backing up his statement by the honour invested in him as a man. But there is no such phrase as "a woman's word," and if we found this phrase somewhere we would correctly surmise that it might well be a euphemism for a lie. Women's honour, Rich argues, has traditionally been based on the private and purely physical relationship of her body to that of her husband and/or family. Women's honour equals chastity: a passive bodily quality. Men's honour, on the other hand, is a lofty sort of thing involving language, the public world, business contracts, wars, and other opportunities for serious thought and moral edification. However, despite the belief that women have no access to the realm of honour, a woman who lies is still blamed for it. We see, then, the ambiguous character of traditional ethical values: they apply to women—sort of—but are primarily meant for males to realize themselves in the world as masculine.

This ambiguity can be seen in the Christian approach to sainthood. A few women might gain access to sainthood by "butch" activities such as theological excellence or holy wars (e.g. Saint Teresa of Avila, Saint Joan of Arc), but these female saints are oddities who were usually persecuted by the Church during their lifetime. The masses of women are supposed to gain access to sainthood by a surfeit of femininity. The paradigm of saintly womanhood is the "virgin and martyr" of the Catholic tradition, who was silent, passive, young, asexual and pure to the bitter end.

The universal values of ethical and moral systems (I will later make a distinction between ethics and morality) have been and still are applicable to women in a derivative and often partial sense. And yet it is crucial to understand these "universal" values and underlying assumptions and see how they act to regulate women's conduct. In other words, it is impossible to completely separate out the purely feminine aspects of our moral experience from those which are shared with men in our specific culture and social group. To understand the concept of female sainthood one has to understand Christian notions of salvation, not just patriarchal notions about women's subservience.

In the building of a counter-morality we will want to pay particular attention to feminine traditions and experiences, as both Rich and Gilligan have done. But there is no such thing as universal feminine experience, even if many of the specifically feminine values of one culture share common elements with the feminine values of another culture. We cannot develop an allegedly universal feminist ethics based on an ethnocentric notion of what is "women's experience." (Later in this chapter I will argue that this is the problem with Mary Daly's philosophy of feminist ethics.)

For instance, the English-speaking maternal feminists of the turn of the century extolled temperance and passionlessness as universal female values, not seeing that these were white, Protestant, middle-class values governing femininity in a specific cultural context. It seems to me that since there is no universal "women's experience" there cannot be a universal women's ethics that would arise directly out of common experience.

Therefore, even though sexual ethics are usually more gender-specific than other areas of moral thought, everything about women's experience cannot be understood with reference only to such gender-specific norms as the double standard. Apart from these, there are notions about sexuality in general that also determine both the institution and the experience of women's ethical conduct. For example, in the Victorian period sexuality was seen as a non-renewable resource and as generally dangerous, while in the twentieth century it is celibacy that is perceived as posing dangers to the health of both men and women.

Having said this, I want to introduce my discussion of feminist sexual ethics with a quick tour of the history of Western sexual ethics as they affect us today, and in particular, how they have affected my own experience and thinking in the realm of sexual ethics.

CHRISTIANITY: THE PURIFICATION OF THE SOUL

When I was seven years old, I was told it was time to prepare to receive my First Communion. I saw this as an important rite of passage, so I willingly participated in the training provided at our school. I'm not sure what we were told about the nature of the Eucharist, but whatever it was, it didn't make much of an impression. But what I clearly remember is the speech a teacher gave us about what our souls had to look like on the day we received Communion. She said: "You will be wearing white dresses, and you'll want to keep them clean and white. But what is even more important is that your souls be white, pure and completely white. Any sins you don't confess are like black stains on your soul, like stains on your beautiful white dresses—and you wouldn't want to have ugly black stains on you on the day of your First Communion, would you?"

Apart from the overt racism of this parable, which didn't strike me at the time, something about it profoundly affected my way of thinking about myself. I suddenly pictured my soul as a white sheet which had to be kept white and never allowed to get dirty, as linen has an unfortunate way of doing.

Prior to this I had had a strong sense of the importance of doing good deeds, such as giving things away to poor children and helping around the house. But the active pursuit of good-ness was suddenly overshadowed by the passive metaphor which told me, "Just keep your soul white, stay still, don't get dirty." Being an active tomboy with a definite knack for get-ting dirty, the task of keeping my soul clean seemed completely overwhelming. And what was purity about? I had enough of a literary sense to know a metaphor when I saw one, but I wasn't sure what the metaphorical whiteness of the soul was. I was not only discouraged, but confused.

Around this same time, I began to indulge in daydreams and fantasies involving Christian saints and martyrs. The priests who came to our school to teach religion were always willing, with a little prodding on our part, to reward us for the tedious task of learning the catechism by heart by telling us gory tales of saints who were sliced to bits with knives for refusing to give up their Christian faith. The pleasure we ob-tained from these sadomasochistic tales was extremely intense, but was sanctified by its religious context. Not surprisingly, my childhood search for pleasure and truth was channelled into fantasies of being tortured by evil men. I imagined that being roasted alive on a grill like Saint Lawrence was similar to getting a bad sunburn. And I thought Saint Catherine's pain on being hacked to death by a wheel of knives was comparable to the pain I suffered when I fell off a bike and got multiple scrapes. So I did not highlight the pain involved in these images. Rather I highlighted my own courage and strength, seeing myself not as a cowering maiden, but as a tough stoic unaf-fected by torture and threats. Yet this was always a *passive* strength. In my fantasies all my emotional resources were marshalled simply to keep my soul from getting stained.

Perhaps this passivity is one of the reasons why Nietzsche accused Christianity of being an effeminate moral framework. The Greeks had a more virile model, in which ethical points were gained by exercising one's faculties fully and properly. Women could not be full ethical beings, at least in the Aristo-telian system, precisely because their social, economic and sexual freedom to act was from the beginning quite limited. They did not have as many opportunities to conduct them-selves ethically by responsibly using their freedom to create personal and political harmony and order. But Christianity, by choosing to cast suspicions on passion per se, regardless of how, when, where and with whom it is expressed, privileged the typically feminine experience of passive preservation of purity as a way to sainthood. And indeed, Christ himself is a rather effeminate figure.

This shows that a moral framework does not have to be virile to be sexist. The exaltation of passive purity tends to encourage passivity, especially female passivity, in the face of injustice. Through the elevation of feminine virtues to the status of universal ethical principles, women are encouraged to see carnal desire (and even intense intellectual desire) as black stains upon the soul. The evil stains may originate in the polluted atmosphere around us, but regardless of their origin, it's our own fault for getting dirty.

The myth of the soul as "whiter than white" laundry prevents us from naming our own desires. Or more accurately, we are given a whole classification system by which to name and grade our passions and sins, not according to our own feelings and thoughts about them but according to a pre-established system.

Before I could take my First Communion, I had to make my first confession. It was in the "training" provided for confession that I became acquainted with the Catholic system for the classification of sins. I was told that there were mortal sins, which would send you straight to hell if you died without having a chance to confess them, and venial sins, which would merely give you time in Purgatory. Apart from that, there were seven "deadly" sins. In respect to these, I was not sure what lasciviousness was, but I worried about committing the sin of gluttony: I loved to eat. Having learned the system, I now worried that when I finished off my sister's half-eaten dinner I might be committing a deadly sin.

The whole system was quite complicated. It was clear that if I was going to make my first confession I would have to engage in a very sophisticated exercise in introspection, classifying not only my sinful actions but even my sinful thoughts, turning my pleasures and fantasies this way and that to see how they fit into the classification system. Although my parents were careful not to expose me to the worst aspects of Catholic sexual guilt, and did not put any perverse thoughts into my head that weren't there already, I definitely got the message, from nuns, priests, and books about holy lives, that sexual passion and pleasures of any sort were a priori suspect.

And yet this whole scheme, which I had thought was firmly implanted in me, went completely out the window as soon as I had opportunities to experience sexual pleasure. I could not see any inherent badness in sex, even sex without love, as long as there was a minimum of mutual respect. I did not feel my desires as blots upon a white soul, but as wonderful new activities that would help me define myself as an adult. Hence, much of my Catholicism went out the window, and I entered the generation of the sexual revolution.

CLASSICAL GREECE: THE ESTHETICS OF EXISTENCE

As I mentioned in chapter one, my adolescence was profoundly marked by a Christian-like struggle with my own body to control the basic desire to eat. Not that I starved myself for the same reasons as Saint Anthony, but my internal struggle resembled Christian mysticism in being shaped by a mistrust of the body and its pleasures. For me, the life of the mind was what was important, and even after I got over the worst part of the anorexia I did not feel very comfortable in my body.

But then I went away to university, abandoning the scene of my rather infantile and regressive battle with myself and my parents about questions of oral eroticism (as a psychoanalyst would say). I left home, found myself a boyfriend, and discovered the joys of adult intellectual conversation at the same time as I discovered the joys of the body. In this time I was seventeen and eighteen, and reading Plato was a crucial step. Opening up his dialogues and expecting to find disembodied and abstract philosophical truths, I was thunderstruck by the amazing interplay of erotic intensity and intellectual depth I found there. "Is this really philosophy?" I wondered. "These people in the dialogue are practically making love as they talk about Truth and Beauty. And they are not at all embarrassed by it!" Compared to later philosophers of the Christian tradition, Plato was a breath, or rather a gust, of fresh air.

For the first time I saw that my own intellectual and erotic passions might be more closely connected than I had previously thought. Eroticism was not just a mute irrational passion, a dark force; it was, so Plato said, part of a holistic ethics and esthetics of human life. Having been brought up without much of a sense that sexual love and the love of truth had anything to do with one another, Plato was a revelation. (Like most young women readers, I always identified with Plato's main characters, completely forgetting that because of my sex the wisdom unfolding before my eyes was not supposed to apply to me. But as women we learn any way we can, especially where pleasure is concerned.)

Although the poets and philosophers of Ancient Greece did indeed subject erotic relations to a great deal of scrutiny, this was based on very different assumptions and methods than the subsequent moral and medical systems of Christian Europe. Erotic energy was not seen as sinful or as opposed to reason. According to Plato, it is precisely through the love of a beautiful body that one begins the long ascent to the philosophic apprehension of Beauty itself. Sexual desire does have to be integrated into the quest for Beauty and Truth, but it is never eliminated or purged, or relegated to the realm of pre-linguistic silence. The question is not how to abolish desire or how to give it external checks, but rather how to let desire grow naturally so that it generates its own internal checks and is in harmony with the other pleasures of human existence, such as the seeking of truth.

Another aspect of classical Greek sexual ethics is the contextual approach, used not only by Plato but even by the much more abstract and pleasureless Aristotle. Neither philosopher tries to decide which sexual acts are by nature wrong or unnatural; indeed, neither thinks of sexual desire in terms of discrete, specific acts that can be scientifically classified. Rather, they try to give the sort of general advice on erotic health that a good health practitioner would give on preventive health. The emphasis is on moderation and on preserving one's inner harmony of desires. There are no fixed penalties for specific sexual acts; rather we are offered reflections on the possible consequences of a certain course of action so that we can act cautiously, paying close attention to the proper time and place for certain pleasures, and to the relationship between those pleasures and the rest of our lives.

This approach is definitely useful in the construction of a feminist ethics or a feminst counter-morality. We are not about to make absolute pronouncements declaring certain sexual activities to be per se bad. Rather, we want to provide women with the intellectual skills to reason about their particular situation, paying close attention to the interconnections between the sexual and the non-sexual aspects of our lives. There is, in my opinion, no feminist tablet of sexual rights and wrongs. But that does not mean we are thrown into total chaos. There are right and wrong ways of thinking about the sexual ethics of concrete situations.

However, I do not want to suggest that the legacy of the Greeks and in particular of Plato is an unmitigated blessing. As Foucault pointed out in his book on Greek sexual ethics, there is an inherent problem in the Greek model which continues to this day to plague our reasoning in sexual matters. The problem lies in the assumption that sexuality, like the management of the household or the government of the city-state, depends on a hierarchy of an active, superior partner and a passive, inferior partner. When the inferior partner is a woman, then her sexual position corresponds to her social position, and no contradiction arises for the system as a whole. But when the "passive" partner is another male, specifically another free male citizen, then a contradiction does arise. How can a young man who has been both wooed and fucked then become the social peer of his lover? How can someone tainted by passivity become part of the ruling groups? The contradiction arises because sexual passivity is assumed to indicate something about a person's social power and a person's very soul. It was also assumed that activity and passivity are rigid and mutually exclusive categories. Even if the two people in question were socially equal prior to having sex, the act of sex is seen as creating a difference, or perhaps revealing an implicit difference, between the active/dominant partner and the passive/submissive partner.

The Greeks, then, set in place the dichotomy of active and passive which continues to plague us today. Living in a hierarchical society, they saw nature in general and human anatomy in particular as necessarily hierarchical, and so interpreted the physical act of penetration as an act of domination. It was the *social* subordination of women, boys and slaves which gave meaning to sex between free adult males and "lower" human beings. Women were not subordinated because they had vaginas; rather, their vaginas were interpreted as the site of rightful domination because women had been previously decreed to be inferior. Male slaves obviously did not have vaginas, and yet their anatomy was interpreted as inherently passive. The social role was thus fundamental, and was used as the basis to arrive at sexual roles.

CONTEMPORARY POP PSYCHOLOGY

I do my thing, and you do your thing
I am not in this world to live up to your expectations
And you are not in this world to live up to mine.
You are you, and I am I,
And if by chance we find each other, it's beautiful.
If not, it can't be helped.

—Fritz Perls

This pseudo-poem is the declaration of independence of the pop psychology of the sixties and seventies. In the austere eighties, this do-your-own-thing approach tends to be moderated, at least among those not in the top 10 percent of the income-earning population, by a recognition of economic and social reality. But even now it continues to exercise a great deal of influence over our lives. The psychologists who followed the lead set by Fritz Perls and Abraham Maslow and went on to make millions by writing books full of banal advice ("You always have some unrealized potential") tried to convince both women and men that since God was dead the only living god was personal success. "Success" no longer had to mean, as it did in the fifties, a traditional nuclear family; it could mean anything from having a good job to having a successful affair. Although the stress was not overtly on material success, the feeling of control over one's own life that was the goal of psychological "growth" was rather difficult if not impossible to attain if one lived in poverty.

The seemingly banal and harmless truth "You are you and I

am I"—who could contradict that?—therefore concealed a distinct political and ethical message. This was not so much a written code of do's and don'ts but a vague and joyous affirmation of the values of urban, consumerist, bourgeois society. Success was interpreted as personal, i.e. individual success. This was not far from the "get ahead" ethic of the fifties, even if it was couched in flowery psychological language.

It is interesting that the famous pseudo-poem quoted above tended to be found on posters with pictures of a young happy couple going off into a Caribbean sunset. The message was thus that even as one individually made one's way in the world without taking other people into account, the "beautiful" ending would indeed happen "by chance," without either partner having to relinquish her/his precious uniqueness. And if it didn't happen by chance, one could always try Club Med.

The young woman looking up at the pseudo-poem emblazoned over the red sunset poster had no way of knowing that its message—that narcissism is compatible with "meaningful" relationships—was meant mainly for men. The new pop psychology tried to be non-sexist; blatant statements about women's inferiority were as passé as the belief in eternal damnation. And it was not that difficult to avoid rigid gender prescriptions, since the whole ethic was so empty of any real ethical content anyway. But the precepts of "do your own thing," and "live and let live," could not be put in practice by the majority of living and breathing female human beings. Real-life women had kids to take care of, bosses whose egos needed constant boosting, and (most) had male sexual partners who would quickly ditch them if they tried to do what was needed for their own personal growth.

Women know this quite well. Yet, although we are well aware that in real life we do not sit atop a mountain surveying the whole world and freely deciding what to do to maximize our personal fulfilment, we continue to believe in the banal and naive slogans of personal growth psychology. Most of us have rejected the rigid frameworks of traditional Christianity; what we have instead is a watered-down version of the romantic ideal of life as one's own unique work of art. We thus often resort to clichés about the inviolability of personal choice and personal desire.

The irony of it all is that we are not very likely to allow *ourselves* any real freedom of choice or permission to do our own thing. We are much better at being understanding about other people's need to "get away for a while" than at allowing ourselves that kind of freedom. This is especially deplorable when women are supremely understanding about their male partner's need for freedom, but are unable to even imagine what they would do if they had similar freedom. I once heard a woman explain very rationally why the man she used to be in a relationship with had found her too demanding and had left her. In my own opinion the man was narcissistic, but she said "I couldn't really blame him; I was too dependent on him; I had no right to expect as much as I did, so of course he resented my expectations and eventually got fed up—I couldn't really blame him."

It is indeed true that blaming the other person is not a useful way of solving problems; but my woman friend was blaming herself, which is hardly an improvement. One wonders who set the parameters of that relationship, who told her, in words or in deeds, that she had virtually no rights. Being deprived of rights tends to increase insecurity, and so might very well have led her to possessiveness. But if she knew she had rights, and was entitled to certain limited but definite expectations, perhaps she would not have sunk into dependence and anxiety. Lacking any framework of responsibility, however, she felt her dependence was her own psychological problem. She saw herself as a deficient being who had not "developed" to the point where she could joyously accept that "if by chance we find each other, it's beautiful, and if not, it can't be helped." As though anyone really felt that way.

The laissez faire approach to sexual relationships might work for people who have numerous opportunities for new relationships and who are young, economically secure, and without major responsibilities to children or to anyone else. And it works for men better than for women, since women are socialized to get more attached to lovers, and to value continuity and security more than spontaneity and novelty. Men, on the other hand, even if their real emotional needs are not that different, are conditioned to think that sexual novelty can make up for the absence of other sources of intimacy. And if sexual novelty is a real possibility, then emotional conflicts and commitments can always be avoided by moving on. As a gay male friend of mine said about the sudden disappearance of a potential lover, "Well, it's like the streetcar. You miss one and get frustrated, but soon enough another one comes along."

It would not be a bad thing if more women began to adopt the streetcar theory, at least for minor flings, and not agonize so much about whether a virtual stranger really likes them or not. As a group, we women tend to turn up the emotional volume on any relationship big or small, rather than take a more relaxed and matter-of-fact approach to sexual liaisons. However, the point is that one cannot very easily go directly from the ideals of lifelong marriage to the streetcar approach. And this is what we are being asked to do by such experts on sexual mores as the fiction writers for *Cosmopolitan*.

The marketplace model is the one most often used by current experts on sexual relationships. The idea is that we are all individuals in a void, and as we wander around in pursuit of our own personal goals of success, fitness and beauty, we run into other atom-like individuals. Then we can pause, compare what each has to offer and, if the two commodities are found to have equal value, the exchange can take place. It tends to be justified according to a theory of psychological compatibility ("We both want the same thing from a relationship," people say). But in fact, socio-economic compatibility is much more to the point. This is apparent from reading such signs of the times as the personal want ads in the *New York Review*. They often leave open-ended the kind of relationship desired, but they are very specific about the kind of person they want. Examples:

"Successful, professional man, handsome and witty, seeks female under 40 who is slender, intelligent, and economically secure, for adventure, fine dining, and possibly more."

"Academic woman with a taste for Bach and the outdoors, pretty and a good conversationalist, seeks a cultivated male, Ph.D. preferred, with similar tastes, for an out-of-the-ordinary liaison. No smokers please."

It is remarkable enough that these people can describe themselves so concisely (and immodestly). But it is even more remarkable that they can know exactly who they want, sight unseen, and can specify the desired sexual object in so much detail. They are undoubtedly the same kind of people who go shopping knowing that they want a pair of maroon corduroy pants with two pleats at the waist and one back pocket—and nothing else will do.

The non-ethics of the pop psychology approach to sexual choices takes the worst from both moral frameworks outlined earlier. From the Greeks it takes the notion of life as a work of art that one works to construct. But it divorces this idea from its roots in the polis, the community. The "beautiful life" sought by the Yuppie generation is not beautiful in the Greek sense of well-proportioned, in harmony with the needs of the wider community, and leading toward truth and goodness. It is "beautiful" in the most banal sense of flashy, impressive, seductive, narcissistic. Pop psychology also takes up the individualism that the Greeks abhorred but which was promoted by the Christian view of virtue as a clean soul that one polishes in splendid isolation. But it no longer requires, as Christianity did, that one back up one's stainless virtue by doing things for others.

We thus have a combination of pseudo-esthetics without its social content and a pseudo-morality also emptied of its content. Lacking any real ethical content, the framework provided by the pop psychology of personal success cannot serve to guide anybody anywhere other than to the dating service, the fitness club and the trendy restaurant. This does not mean that the people using these services for Yuppies are necessarily devoid of ethical sense or values. But insofar as they have any values other than to consume well, these have to come from outside the social framework in which they live. Some of them therefore hold on to old-fashioned Christian values; some take up EST or a watered-down version of Eastern religion; others have a commitment to feminism or to other progressive social movements. But the prevailing culture of urban, white, young professionals and would-be professionals does not itself have any ethical content. It forces those people who do have a strong ethical sense to arbitrarily choose values and standards from any place they can. No wonder there is so much confusion about sexual liberation.

FEMINIST ALTERNATIVES

No one feminist today can invent a complete feminist ethical system. Nor would this in any case be desirable, since any feminist theory of social relations must have a sense of flexibility, pluralism, and respect for individual and group differences. If and when a feminist ethics is developed, it will resemble the Greek discussions of general principles for a harmonious life more than a closed theological system of right and wrong. And given the lack of consensus, even among feminists, about the ethics and politics of sexuality, even general principles are not going to be easy to develop. All that any one writer can do is reflect on the collective experience and thoughts of women who are trying to develop a new ethical code that goes beyond both patriarchal extremes of rigid authoritarianism and vapid libertarianism. From this, the writer can try to indicate some of the pitfalls to be avoided and some of the more promising avenues for further reflection and praxis. This is what I will attempt in this last section of the book. The emphasis is not on any "correct" answers, but rather on the questions.

Reading the current heated feminist debates about sexuality, women who do not have a strong position one way or another or who are new to feminism are sometimes discouraged and puzzled. Why is there so much infighting, they ask. If as feminists we all agree about equal pay, abortion rights, childcare and sexual assault, why do we have to bicker so much about sexuality? And will the movement not come to grief if we argue so much?

Anyone worried by these questions would do well to remember that the women's movement has *never* agreed about sexual ethics, and that it has managed to survive as a viable historical force and to make certain concrete gains even as disagreement continued in some areas of feminist thought. In 1914 the British feminist Rebecca West argued passionately against the "maternal feminism" advocated by many suffragists. They considered passion and lust to be peculiarly male, and emphasized women's capacity to nurture rather than their capacity for pleasure. Yet even as she denounced the maternal feminists' notion of specifically feminine values and advocated women's intellectual and sexual *equality* with men, she still went on all the suffrage demonstrations. She fought alongside the maternal feminists for the vote and for better jobs for women. Then as now, feminism was broad enough to contain different philosophical frameworks and different lifestyles. The critical examinations of various positions on sexual ethics that I undertake here are thus not designed to throw anyone out of the movement, but only to point out the very different assumptions that underlie these differences and to reflect on the political and personal consequences that follow from them.

Mary Daly: the moral superiority of natural womanhood

Some radical feminist writers, particularly in the United States, have tried to elaborate an alternative ethical vision based on women's specifically feminine experience. Patriarchal society, they argue, is based on misogyny, violence against women, and the mindless pursuit of pleasure, even when these goals are legitimated by appeals to religion, patriotism, or other ideological systems. So the feminist challenge to patriarchy has to recuperate the feminine values and experiences and not fall into the trap of advocating that women become equal with men. These radical feminists are the descendants of the maternal feminists of the turn of the century, although they tend to be more critical of marriage and the traditional family. Susan Griffin, Robin Morgan, Andrea Dworkin and Mary Daly are some of the main spokespersons for this view. In what follows I will concentrate primarily on Mary Daly, whose work is more explicitly philosophical and ethical than that of the others.

Mary Daly explains as follows her project of developing a feminist philosophy that would include a theory of ethics as well as a theory of knowledge and a metaphysics:

The work of such complex Naming [i.e. theorizing] is an in-vocation of Other reality. It is an invitation to the country of the Strange. For the Strange is the homeland of women who identify as women, and Wild Women are Strange. This work, insofar as it is an expression/expansion of Pure Lust, is a con-juring of the Elemental Spirits of women and all Wild natures. Such conjuring conjoins women with our Selves and with our Sisters, and with earth, air, fire, and water. It connects us with the rhythms of the farthest stars and of our own sun and moon.[3]

And a little further, she adds:

A basic thesis of this book, implied in the title, is that women . . . . are rooted, as are animals and trees, in the Earth's sub-stance. . . . the Race of Women is Wild and Tidal, roaring with rhythms that are elemental, that are created in cosmic encounters.[4]

The language chosen by Daly to describe women's roots in Nature is purposefully vague. She argues elsewhere that she is not interested in male, goal-directed, systematic thought, and that she would rather use metaphors than facts and logical arguments. However, even if one grants her the right to use whatever language and logic she likes, it remains unclear how we are to interpret certain statements. What does she mean when she says that the rhythms of the "Race of Women" are "created in cosmic encounters"? Encounters between what and what? Poetic language is fine when one wants to create powerful images, but if one is trying to build a philosophical system and argue that these images are a *true* picture of how things are or should be, the vagueness becomes a serious prob-lem. As we shall see, the seemingly descriptive phrases about elemental rhythms later become prescriptions for how we should behave as feminists. Real feminists are separated from what she calls "male controlled pseudofeminism" (p. 112). She avoids giving examples of "pseudofeminism," so that the reader becomes anxious and wonders if *her* feminist soul has been stained by pseudofeminism.

But what are the characteristics of what Daly calls, in the subtitle of her latest book, "elemental feminist philosophy"? It is evident in the passages quoted above that she believes women are a "Race." That is, women have a common bio-logical and social identity and a common destiny. This identity is for Daly always a stronger bond than nationality, class, or "race" in the usual sense of the word. Class and nationality are not discussed at all. For Daly they are simply unfortunate and unimportant obstacles in the way of creating a transnational sisterhood. And she claims that racism is just a manifestation of patriarchy, and so by fighting against patriarchy one is automatically fighting racism. But she simply states this point without proving or even arguing for it. That black feminists have argued until they are hoarse that racism is *not* just an offshoot of patriarchy, and that black women have an allegiance not just to other women in general but to other black people both male and female, is not taken into consideration. The very phrase "Race of Women" is offensive to women of colour, both because it denies their commitment to their own race and because it attempts to create a pre-given identity among all women. As black feminist Bell Hooks has argued, sisterhood is not a fact, but a complicated process that feminists can work toward once they come to grips with the profound differences among women.[5]

This is relevant to sexual ethics since cultural, ethnic and religious differences among women will continue to influence our approach to sexuality and to relationships. There is no such thing as "women's experience" in general. A single mother in Jamaica, a lesbian feminist in New York, a married white woman in South Africa, and a Chinese teenage girl all have different experiences and attitudes. These cannot be dismissed simply because all the women in question live in male-dominated societies. Male domination takes very different forms in different places and in different social classes. And in any case, it is naive to assume that if male domination did not exist all women would think and act alike.

Because there is no general "women's experience," those who hold this view have arbitrary choices about what will or will not count as valid female experience. Mary Daly chooses those elements of patriarchal thought which associate women with Nature, the elements, the rhythms of the moon, plants and animals and everything that is not rational or artificial. So these ideologically constructed images of womanhood are adapted for feminist use.

Other traditional images of womanhood, notably those symbolizing passivity and devotion to men and children, are rejected. This rejection is more or less standard among feminists, since one thing we have in common is an attempt to affirm women's autonomy and active power. But having rejected these, why should we continue to believe in the equally traditional images of women in touch with the rhythms of the moon? Why assume that the moon, the stars and the tides are female? Why not computers, spaceships and abstract art? That the domination of women in Western societies is closely linked to the domination of Nature is no reason to assume that women are *in fact* closer to Nature. As feminists we want to have a non-instrumental, healthier relationship to Nature than that of plunder and ecological disaster. But this rational attitude is not rooted in our primeval connection to the rhythms of the moon. We don't *intuit* that oil spills are bad for the planet; we reason it, and use facts to prove it. If women did rely only on intuition, how would men ever have a chance to reform their own relationship to Nature? The view that women are more "natural" than men lets men off the hook quite nicely. For if men are massacring the planet because they are men, they can't really help it and it has to be women who save the planet.

This view of women as close to Nature presents some serious problems. Mary Daly does not directly address the issue of sexuality (despite the title, *Pure Lust*, sex is never mentioned) but she does lay the groundwork for a particular kind of sexual ethics in her philosophy. On the first page of her book she states that "Phallic lust is seen as a fusion of obsession and aggression," involving "genital fixation and fetishism." By contrast, "elemental female Lust" has nothing to do with the genitals:

> Elemental female Lust is intense longing/craving for the cosmic concrescence that is creation. It is charged, tense, in tension with the tenses of fabricated 'father time'. Incensed, it burns through the shallow impressions of insipid senses, sensing the Sources, Astral Forces, Angels and Graces that call from the Deep.[6]

Women's desire is, in Daly's opinion, a desire not for sex but for "creation," Nature as created by Spirit. The choice of the word "creation" is interesting, especially by a writer who is so careful about what words she uses. Creation is Nature as seen from the point of view of God. Now, Daly no longer believes in a patriarchal God, but she most definitely believes in Spirit, "the Sources, Astral Forces, Angels and Graces." She also believes that the spiritual realm is more important, more fundamental, and ultimately more real than the world of the "insipid senses." Daly dedicates her book "To the Spirit/who lives and breathes/in all Elemental be-ing," and then says that this spirit is only inadequately represented in mythic female images. Elsewhere she states that words are inadequate to express feminist philosophy.

Well, this sounds suspiciously like Catholic theology with a feminist bent to me. And if Daly wants to remain within the Catholic framework, substituting a feminine Spirit for a patriarchal God, that is of course her right. But what I object to is her presentation of her beliefs as *the* truth, as "elemental feminist philosophy." It's not philosophy; it's religion.

Like all religious thinkers, Daly is uncomfortable with the body in general and with sex in particular. When she rejects "phallic lust," one has to agree with her that the violent and fetishistic aspects of masculine sexuality as presently constructed are not something we want to keep. But she does not differentiate between male sexuality and the social construction of masculinity. The impression is created that men are *by nature* violent and fetishistic in their sexuality. The description of "phallic lust" is not followed by an account of how men are pressured into adopting such a sexuality, or by an explanation of how men might express their lust differently in a different society.

It could be argued that feminists are not about to waste their time reforming male sexuality. But if we do not understand how masculine, as opposed to male, sexuality is organized we will have no criterion for evaluating different male sexual practices or perhaps more to the point, for constructively criticizing our own heterosexual relationships. The "take it or leave it" approach prevents women from finding the weak links, the pressure points that can be used to transform and subvert heterosexuality.

In fact, Daly's account of men's "phallic lust" and women's "pure" lust makes heterosexuality *necessarily* anti-feminist and bad for women. In this she closely resembles Andrea Dworkin. She assumes that in any and all connections between men and women, men drain women's elemental energies and power. Both in her earlier work, *Gyn/Ecology* and in *Pure Lust*, metaphors about Dracula and about vampires abound. These suggest that women are inherently victims and that men are so empty of vital energies that the only way they can live is by drawing off women's blood. Heterosexuality is often, or even most of the time, an unequal exchange in which women give a lot more than they get. But to convey this through the static and mythical image of vampirism precludes the possibility of transforming heterosexuality. In the vampire movies, the female victim remains a victim, and the vampire remains a vampire. But heterosexuality is, as we argued earlier, a social process subject to historical transformation.

The dismissal of heterosexuality does not necessarily bring with it an affirmation of lesbianism. Daly prefers to talk about spiritual bonding between women rather than about sex between women. We saw before that "elemental female lust" was described as a mythical apprehension of the unity of Nature, in a basically Christian context. This is not very far from the old idea that women do not want sex, they just want love. It is also very similar to Plato's idea that true love is not love of an individual body but of the Idea of Beauty itself. Daly states that physical intimacy is an "obsession" of "phallic lust" (p. 80), and that real feminists are instead interested in what she calls "physical ultimacy." "Ultimacy" is never defined, but we are told it has nothing to do with "casual or pseudo-intense 'relationships'".

So, heterosexuality is forbidden to real feminists, and yet lesbianism is so desexualized that one would mistake Daly's descriptions of feminist communities for descriptions of medieval nunneries. Not only that, but women who enjoy physical intimacy are tainted with patriarchy. They may enjoy their relationships, but Daly dismisses them, sight unseen, as "casual or pseudo-intense." (Why are they necessarily pseudo-intense? Because they involve sex and not pure spirit?)

In conclusion, Daly's attempt to build a feminist ethics takes us into dangerous territory. First, we are supposed to adhere to a rigid notion of what is and is not female or feminine. Racial, national and class conflicts between women are swept under the carpet, and there is no recognition that not all women necessarily feel at home in the Eternal Feminine of Western philosophy and theology. Further, women's sexuality is channelled exclusively in a spiritual direction. Although Daly does not state it in so many words (since she dislikes the very word "sex"), one gets the impression that heterosexuality is completely forbidden, lesbianism is tolerated only if firmly inscribed in an elemental lust for creation, and celibacy is the highest good. In general her whole philosophy tries to prevent any principled disagreements and real differences among feminists from even being discussed.

A frightening example of this authoritarian tendency is found in *Pure Lust*, where Daly dismisses the Third World feminists who attended the UN Conference on Women held in Copenhagen in 1980 as "male-identified," disregarding what women's liberation means to women in underdeveloped parts of the world. She tries to *force* her notion of sisterhood-at-all-costs onto everyone else by saying, "*Women* are raped, beaten, maimed, killed and dismembered by *males* of all nations, classes, races, in all times and places. . . ."[7] An ahistorical notion of patriarchy is thus used to suppress the acknowledgment of other forms of oppression, and to hide the conflicts of interest between the women who pick coffee beans for fifty cents a day in Brazil and the white American feminist who sips coffee as she writes about women in general. By means of this ahistorical and almost mystical notion of patriarchy, women who say "But what if we *like* fucking?" can be thrown out of church for disrespect and lack of that essential Daly requirement of "faith."[8]

The reaction to naturalism: talking sex

Some contemporary feminists have criticized the ideas developed by Mary Daly and by such anti-pornography writers as

Andrea Dworkin for reflecting an old-fashioned dislike or fear of sex itself, especially unconventional sex. They deplore the fact that sexual liberation has been put way down on the agenda of the women's movement—or, by Daly and Dworkin, more or less struck off altogether—while a lot has been made of women's victimization by men, by male violence, and by pornography. These feminists want to bring back sexual liberation as a feminist issue.

An important book that gathered the writings of many American feminists involved in this counter-attack was significantly entitled *Pleasure and Danger: Exploring Women's Sexuality*,[9] and it was no coincidence that although violence against women and other dangerous aspects of sex were acknowledged, pleasure was first on the title. While some of the contributors to this anthology maintained a good balance between recuperating sexual liberation and acknowledging the problems inherent in male-defined sexual freedom, it was unfortunate (though probably inevitable) that others took a polemical stance, rejecting the moralism of Mary Daly only to embrace a sexual libertarianism that was out of step with the experiences of most women. Some of the contributors had been trashed quite harshly and denounced as male-identified by anti-porn feminists, and it was natural that they would react by loudly proclaiming their right to be "bad girls" if so they chose. Certainly, after a dose of Mary Daly one is tempted to revert precisely to the status of "bad girl," just to spite the holy maternal figure of authority.

Although for some "pro-sex" feminists sexual liberation was defined as a process guided by feminist values and differentiated carefully from the Playboy ideology, others saw sexual liberation as having only one ethical value: consent. Gayle Rubin, whose piece "Thinking Sex" was the most substantial in the *Pleasure and Danger* anthology, took the position that the only judgement to be made about sexual activity was whether or not it was consensual. And if the people involved consented, no further questions need be posed. She also presented a rather skewed review of the history of sexuality in the West. "Sex negativity" was presented as the main feature of Western thought about sex, as though gender oppression were a merely incidental factor and sex an undifferentiated whole that one could be for or against.

As feminists we know that consent is relative, since people are not equally informed and equally powerful and do not necessarily have many choices. Rubin's exclusive focus on consent reminds me of a man I recently saw pushing his way across a picket line of bookstore clerks on strike for their first contract: "Well, why don't you get a better job?" he said, as he was informed that they were on strike because they only earned $4.50 an hour. The workers were "consenting" to being exploited, but only for their lack of alternatives, so it was exploitation nevertheless. And the woman who has been brought up to ignore her own sexual feelings and to let men "bring her alive sexually" might "consent" to all kinds of sexual acts that she has never experienced a desire for—again because she has not learned to imagine for herself.

The idea of consent is of course crucial to any feminist sexual ethics. But the point is that we are not autonomous individuals with equal amounts of power. Therefore the notion of consent cannot suffice to build a sexual ethic, for information and power are necessary preconditions of true consent.

There is another aspect of feminist sexual libertarianism that can lead to problems, especially in the context of trying to develop an ethics of sexuality. This is found both in the Gayle Rubin essay referred to above, and in other essays in the same anthology, such as Paula Webster's "The Forbidden: Eroticism and Taboo."

Webster's article is a plea for women to talk about their desires, let down their inhibitions, and to go ahead and break as many taboos as they like without being afraid of judgements. This talking process is seen as liberating in itself, regardless of the content of our desires/fantasies. The point is to challenge the taboos that inhibit our sexuality. By disregarding taboos—both those inherited from family and tradition and those imposed by dogmatic feminist notions of politically correct sex—we will be able to achieve, Webster argues, "sexual autonomy."

It is of course crucial that we learn to speak about our desires, and that we exercise our imagination in our sexual lives. The weight of tradition, inhibition and guilt has to be constantly thrown off; even those of us who are relatively "liberated" in our sexual practices on occasion suffer from irrational guilt or from a fear of what will happen if we speak our desire out loud. Learning to overcome shame, accepting that there are no right and wrong ways to make love, is important indeed.

However, we must not exaggerate the importance of "talking sex." We must be conscious of the problems caused by the confessional form, as described in the introduction. Webster's article seems to me caught up in the titillation of confessionalism, in the pleasure of speaking "the forbidden" and breaking one taboo after another, without any sense that this practice remains trapped in the framework that we have inherited. There is not much creativity in the constant breaking of taboos, for it does not in itself entail an examination of why certain things are taboos and not others. We are not any freer from the old morality than those who respect taboos.

This framework does not allow us to distinguish between desires, nor does it give us criteria by which we can evaluate them. If a woman truly wants to wear high heels and a corset and be tied to her bed by a macho man in cowboy boots, we are not given a way to understand her "honest" desire as being socially instilled. I certainly would not want to "shame" this woman or tell her not to do what she wants to do. But I would not call her activity part of women's liberation. The content of her desire was produced by sexism. In enacting it she is perhaps being "a naughty girl" and challenging Puritanism, but gender relations remain intact. We need a framework that allows us to understand why women do indeed feel certain desires and not others, and what the political and social implications of various desires might be. This does not imply passing judgement on anyone's sexual life. Understanding the social roots of desire does not necessitate a dogmatic paradigm of what is or is not politically correct, a feminist list of do's and don'ts.

Underlying this "talking sex" idea is a view of sexual identity as an autonomous, individual force constantly held in check by social constraint. This view reduces liberation to individual autonomy. But if sexuality is, as we have argued throughout this book, a social and collective process as well as an individual identity, then individual freedom to imagine and to act is not enough. The notion of individual autonomy tends to make each individual into an isolated fortress. It hinders the development of community discussions about sexual ethics and about the relationship between sexual life and other aspects of our lives. If we start criticizing traditional morality only to fall back into an empty notion of the inviolability of individual desire, we will have no tools for analyzing why a white man might want to turn a black woman into his sexual slave, or why a black woman might "consent" to this.

Sexual desire is not like a reservoir of water contained by the dam of social constraint. Sexuality is constructed by social forces, shaped by the individual's experiences and beliefs, and is always in the process of changing. To liberate our desire is not as simple as breaking the dam; it involves trying to get away from the repression/freedom dichotomy altogether in order to *build* our own sexuality. This building is not an individual matter; the culture around us, our sexual partners, our friends, and our political values are all involved in the process. We all integrate these influences and ideas as best we can, guided by our own sense of what is pleasurable and what is ethical.

If we limit our discussion in groups to talking about fantasies and desires, we run the risk of simply giving voice to a few well-worn clichés: "I want to be raped by a man with a huge penis"; "I want to put on black leather boots and whip another woman." Talking sex has to be creative as well as uninhibited. In this talking/creating process, what may come to mind most readily and turn us on most immediately, is precisely a softcore pornographic cliché. We don't have to recoil in horror or feel ashamed; we might choose to act it out to see what it feels like. But we could try to subvert these scenarios even in acting them out—by reversing conventional symbols, by adding our own original touch to the scenario, or simply by refusing to take these fantasies too seriously. A good giggle goes a long way in challenging the power of patriarchal imagery.

Thus, the main problems inherent in feminist sexual liberationism are all due to an over-emphasis on individual autonomy. If we assume everyone is autonomous and equal, then we will have to believe that the market is fair and everyone is getting what she/he wants. Consent is the only ethical value in this laissez faire view of sexual relations. By contrast, a critique of the distribution of social power could lead us to a more cautious and integrated view of sexual power, which would look at what exactly is involved when women consent to an act which does not originate with them. It would also not assume that once consent has been established there are no more questions to be asked. Individual morality suggests that sexual coercion is clearly wrong; but, as I will argue in a minute, only community ethics can suggest what is right.

A less individualistic view of sexuality would also not elevate sexual autonomy (whatever that would be!) to the status of an absolute value. Rather it would involve analyzing how our sexuality is shaped by communal forces, such as gender, race, and class relations of domination, and discovering how we might undermine these relations of domination in our sexual life. Sexuality, in other words, is a social process that forms one aspect of our lives as women. It is not a ready-made force lurking in the primeval depths of our feminine being. Rather, we build our sexuality as we go along—not out of nothing, not in splendid individual autonomy, but in the same way as we develop our political sense and our literary imagination, that is, as members of certain groups that both inherit certain traditions and resist them. We are trying to create a sexual culture of resistance, which is an integral part of the feminist project.

FEMINIST ETHICS, FEMINIST PLEASURES

It would be a contradiction in terms to develop a "feminist morality," a code of rights and wrongs based on some arbitrary notion of individual feminist virtue. But while the term "morality" suggests both rigidity and individualism, the term "ethics" is more suited to the kind of approach that feminists need. Ethics connotes reasoning about values and actions; it connotes discussion and community. Ethics also suggests the developing of guidelines, and not so much the drawing up of a rigid code that would substitute for the process of reasoning and discussion.

A feminist sexual ethics would be based on the recognition

of sexual diversity. It would not assume that long-term monogamous relationships are the only ones that can be ethical, and it would not privilege certain forms of sexual activity over others. It would try to come up with criteria for discussing ethical behaviour within the framework set by those who practice a particular form of sexuality. For instance, it would not assume that the rules governing self-defined monogamous relationships could be transferred to a group of people who do not see "faithfulness" as a value, but who still want to maintain a sense of commitment and responsibility. As Lorna Weir and Leo Casey put it, the task at hand is to allow for and try to build "a multiplicity of ethical sexualities. . . . A position that respects sexual diversity and examines the social construction of various sexual discourses and practices without pre-given norms and hierarchies does not necessarily lead to moral nihilism."[10]

Some people might argue that regardless of how flexible our new feminist ethics might be, there is still a basic contradiction between the requirements of ethical behaviour and everything we have developed in this book about the need for women to explore and develop sexual pleasure. Put simply, ethics is about responsibility to others, while pleasure is about doing what one wants.

If we see pleasure as individualistic and apolitical, as the bursting forth of dark inner forces, then of course it will be difficult to integrate pleasure and ethics. But this is not how desire and pleasure need to be understood or experienced. As stated in the chapter on desire, it is mythical to see desire as an irrational, destructive force emanating from somewhere within the individual ego, and which knows no boundaries except those imposed on it from the outside by morality, the law, or the super-ego. Desire does not have to be destructive, and power in sexuality does not have to mean humiliation. Power can be understood as inhering not in the selfish "dark" part of one's soul but as a process resulting from interaction among people who are doing something together. Desire for pleasure can include a desire for community, a desire to give as well as to get pleasure, a desire for a more ethical world.

Conversely, if ethics is not a staid system imposed on us from outside, and if it is the result of our own discussions and reflections, then we can feel it as truly *ours*. It can be a set of values or guidelines that *we* have helped to develop and to which we have a commitment. Ethical and political values can be the objects of our desire.

Some tension, however, will always remain between pleasure and ethics. There are times when you get a crush on your best friend's lover, and you have to resort to self-discipline, Christian-style, in order to turn away from the object of your desire. There are times when you feel like being completely irresponsible and having sex with the first person that crosses your path, even though you know you are doing that to avoid struggling with your lover through a conflict.

But the tension between pleasure and ethics does not amount to an absolute contradiction. There are times when the two aspects of our life come together in a very powerful way, and in those times we get a glimpse of what it might be like to live in a post-patriarchal, post-individualistic society. For me, those moments are important reminders of what being a social creature is all about. They suggest that we do not always have to sacrifice pleasure for virtue or vice-versa. One example that comes to mind has to do with a difficult sexual situation that I was in for quite some time. I was the lover of a woman who had another regular lover. Both her other lover and I experienced jealousy and dejection at various times. Yet there were times when all that vanished, and we felt a disinterested affection for one another, rooted in a sense of common purpose. We felt pleasure in putting our political ideals into practice. Those moments gave me a particularly peaceful, quiet kind of pleasure that was very different from the goal-directed, more personal pleasure of getting what we want regardless of others' needs and wants. At those moments, desire and ethical and political ideals were in harmony with one another. My desire for my lover was, at least for a time, not exclusive or selfish, and it was heightened, not diminished, by my awareness of "the other" desire between her and her other lover.

This is not to diminish the significance of conflicts or minimize the problems involved in sexual relations in today's world. But it is to suggest that conflicts do not have to lead to stagnation and misery. The conflicts among different desires, and between desire and ethics, can be creative ones that lead us a little closer to a caring community which can both guide us and provide a context for our desire.

Sexual desire will always have a wild, lawless element. But in a more cohesive and more enlightened community, in which values can be discussed without moralism, this desire would be experienced differently. We would not have to go around feeling like powder-kegs of raw desire. And we would not feel constant opposition between our own desires and those of our friends and lovers. The conflicts between people, and the tension between responsibility and pleasure, would take place in a context that allowed for the resolution, or at least the clarification, of conflicts.

There is no doubt, however, that as long as we live in a consumerist, competitive world in which a certain gender and class hog power and use it against others our sexual relations cannot be fully transformed. We will stumble along, experiencing occasional moments of clarity and peace that give us a sense of what could be possible, and generally trying to do the best we can to reconcile our need for sensual pleasure with our passion for ethical and political pleasure. A full transformation of our sexuality can only take place in a society that is as a whole challenging the patriarchal legacies of our past, and in which real, functioning communities balance and guide individual desire.

♦

NOTES

INTRODUCTION

1 The word sexuality was introduced into the English language around 1800, but it was only in the last two decades of the century that it gained any prominence. For more on the significance of this term, see Michel Foucault, *The History of Sexuality Volume I: An Introduction* (New York, Pantheon, 1978), and Jeffrey Weeks, *Sex, Politics and Society* (London, Longman, 1981).

2 The sexual politics of the first wave of the women's movement have not been studied very much; but see Judith Walkowitz, *Prostitution and Victorian Society* (Cambridge Univ. Press, 1980).

3 This was also a problem for the feminists and homosexuals of the 1918-1939 period of sexual/political activity. The most notable example of the internalization of sexological models is Radclyffe Hall's *The Well of Loneliness*, the "classic novel of lesbian love" published in 1928.

4 Susan Brownmiller, *Against Our Will: Men, Women and Rape* (New York, Bantam, 1975).

5 Andrea Dworkin, *Pornography: Men Possessing Women* (New York, Perigee, 1979). In this book Dworkin even reduces financial power to male power, saying that "money is male power," as though the two forms of power could never exist separately, or as though women could never exercise financial power over other women without thereby becoming male.

6 Muriel Dimen, "Politically Correct? Politically Incorrect?" in Carole Vance, ed., *Pleasure and Danger: Exploring Female Sexuality* (London and Boston, Routledge and Kegan Paul, 1984), p. 141. This line of argument has been developed in the United States by Gayle Rubin and Pat Califia.

7 In the anthology mentioned in the previous footnote, Gayle Rubin dismisses the approach used in this book as a weak-kneed attempt to stay in the middle of the debate without going to either extreme. She thus "explains" various positions only by reference to how daring one is in negating conventional morality, a criterion that assumes that the breaking of taboos is in and of itself a worthwhile activity. Daring people are not always correct, however, or thoughtful about their daring. See her article "Thinking Sex," especially pages 303-309, in *Pleasure and Danger*.

---

8 Audre Lorde, "Uses of the erotic: The erotic as power" in L. Lederer, ed., *Take Back the Night: Women on Pornography* (New York, Bantam, 1980), pp. 295-300.

9 See especially Adrienne Rich's *Twenty-One Love Poems* (collected in *The Dream of a Common Language*, New York, Norton, 1978). In this group of poems, which opens with a description of the lesbian/poet walking through the city of pornography and horror, Rich manages to provide descriptions of sexual love that are both startlingly graphic and movingly beautiful.
For Rich's critique of motherhood as an ideology, see her *Of Woman Born* (New York, Bantam, 1976).

10 S. Cartledge and J. Ryan, eds., *Sex and Love: New Thoughts on Old Contradictions* (London, Women's Press, 1983); and Varda Burstyn, ed., *Women Against Censorship* (Toronto: Douglas and McIntyre, 1984).

11 Kate Millett, *Sita* (New York, Ballantine, 1976).

12 Michel Foucault, op. cit.

CHAPTER ONE

1 The best critique of this contemporary view of sexuality as the truth about people has been carried out by Michel Foucault, *History of Sexuality Volume I: An Introduction* (New York, Pantheon, 1978).

2 Paul Robinson, *The Modernization of Sex* (New York, Harper and Row, 1976).

3 See Jessica Benjamin, "Master and Slave: The Fantasy of Erotic Domination," in A. Snitow, C. Stansell and S. Thompson, *Powers of Desire* (New York, Monthly Review, 1982). My adaptation of the Hegelian master/slave dialectic is somewhat different than Benjamin's.

4 Nancy Chodorow, *The Reproduction of Mothering* (Berkeley, Univ. of Calif., 1978).
See also Dorothy Dinnerstein, *The Mermaid and the Minotaur* (New York, Harper and Row, 1977).

5 For an analysis of masochism, see chapter six.

6 My analysis is, like Jessica Benjamin's, loosely based on Hegel's account of the master/slave dialectic, in which the master is defeated precisely because his very victory robs him of a potential Other who can recognize him. Hegel's account in the *Phenomenology of the Spirit* is nearly impenetrable; but see A. Kojève, *Introduction to the Reading of Hegel* (New York, Basic Books, 1969), for an enlightening if somewhat idiosyncratic commentary.

CHAPTER TWO

1 Joyce Brothers, *What Every Woman Should Know About Men* (New York, Ballantine, 1981), p. 178.

2 See for instance Ruth Bleier, *Science and Gender* (New York, Pergammon, 1984), especially chapter five on human evolution. See also Eleanor Leacock, "Women in Egalitarian Societies," in R. Bridenthal and C. Koonz, eds., *Becoming Visible* (Boston, Houghton Mifflin, 1977).

3 Shere Hite, *The Hite Report* (New York, Dell, 1976).

4 Simone de Beauvoir, *The Second Sex*, H.M. Parshley, trans. and ed. (New York, Random House, 1974), pp. 167-169.

5 Ibid., p. 172.

6 See for instance Karen Horney's discussion of the "male dread of women," in *Feminine Psychology* (New York, Norton, 1967).

7 Sigmund Freud, "Femininity" (from the Introductory Lectures), reprinted in A. Jaggar and P. Rothenberg, *Feminist Frameworks* (New York, McGraw-Hill, 1984), p. 93.

8 Angela Hamblin, "Is Feminist Heterosexuality Possible?", in S. Cartlede and J. Ryan, eds., *Sex and Love* (London, Women's Press, 1983), p. 105.

9 Ibid., p. 113.

CHAPTER THREE

1 Radclyffe Hall, *The Well of Loneliness* (London, Corgi, 1968; orig. publ. Jonathan Cape, 1928), pp. 234-235.

2 Lillian Faderman, *Surpassing the Love of Men: Romantic Friendships and Love Between Women* (New York, Morrow, 1981).

3 Caroll Smith-Rosenberg, "The Female World of Love and Ritual: Relations between women in 19th century America," *Signs*, vol. 1 no. 1, (1975), pp. 1-29.

4 Lillian Faderman, *Lesbian Feminism in Turn-of-the-Century Germany* (Weatherby Lake, Miss., Naiad Press, 1980).

5 Elaine Showalter, ed., *These Modern Women: Autobiographical Essays from Women in the Twenties* (New York, Feminist Press, 1978).

6 Dolores Hayden, *The Grand Domestic Revolution* (Cambridge, MIT Press, 1981).

7 Linda Gordon, *Woman's Body, Woman's Right: A History of Birth Control in America* (New York, Penguin, 1977), p. 202.

8 Adrienne Rich, "Compulsory Heterosexuality and Lesbian Existence," *Signs: A Journal of Women in Society*, vol. 5, no. 4 (Summer 1980).

9 M.A. Jensen, *Love's Sweet Return: The Harlequin Story* (Toronto, Women's Press, 1983), p. 100.

10 Adrienne Rich, *The Dream of a Common Language* (New York, Norton, 1978), p. 31.

11 Quentin Bell, *Virginia Woolf: A Biography* (New York, Harcourt Brace Jovanovich, 1972); 2 vols. Victoria Glendinning, *Vita* (New York, Knopf, 1983). For a different perspective, see Louise de Salvo, "Lighting the Cave: The Relationship between Vita Sackville-West and Virginia Woolf," in *Signs*, vol. 8, no. 2 (Winter 1982), pp. 195-214.

12 An interesting autobiographical account of such a triangle is found in Mary Meigs, *The Medusa Head* (Vancouver, Talon books, 1983).

13 Recently, the North American lesbian community was rocked by a publishing scandal that threatened to blur the previously clear separation between "lesbian" porn and lesbian culture. This took place when *Penthouse*'s Bob Guccione bought the rights to reprint excerpts of a book about lesbian nuns, published by the lesbian feminist Naiad Press, for his other publication, *Forum*. Some of the nuns and ex-nuns who contributed their personal stories to the book were horrified to see their words turned into pornography so as to generate profits for Guccione. This case will be analyzed in the next chapter, since it illustrates some of the problems inherent in mainstream feminist definitions of pornography.

14 Lorna Weir and Leo Casey, "Subverting Power in Sexuality," *Socialist Review*, No. 75-76, p. 152.

CHAPTER FOUR

1 Adrienne Rich, "Compulsory Heterosexuality and Lesbian Existence," *Signs: A Journal of Women in Society* vol. 5, no. 4 (Summer 1980).

CHAPTER FIVE

1 See my article in C. Guberman and M. Wolfe, eds., *No Safe Place: Violence Against Women and Children* (Toronto, Women's Press, 1985), which explores in more depth many of the issues raised in this chapter.

2 R. Curb and N. Monahan, *Lesbian Nuns: Breaking Silence* (Naiad, 1985).

3 Reasonably reliable statistics on the consumption of pornography in Canada can be found in the Badgley *Report on Sexual Offences Against Children* (Govt. of Canada, Nov. 1984), vol. II, pp. 1214-1279.

4 The "holy family" analogy is borrowed from Ruby Rich's critique of *Not a Love Story*—see B. Ruby Rich, "Anti-Porn: Soft Issue, hard world," *The Village Voice*, July 20, 1982.

5 For a critique of the traditional feminist concept of "objectification," see Lorna Weir and Leo Casey, "Subverting Power in Sexuality," *Socialist Review* No. 75-76 (May-Aug. 1984), pp. 139-158.

6 In Canada, see back issues of *Fuse* magazine, a cultural publication which has published important articles on feminist art and the problems of censorship. See also Varda Burstyn, ed., *Women Against Censorship* (Toronto, Douglas and McIntyre, 1985).

CHAPTER SIX

1 Norbert Elias, *The History of Manners* (New York, Pantheon, 1978). This is the first volume of a two-volume history of the notions of "culture" and "civilization."

2 Joanna Russ, "Somebody is trying to kill me and I think it's my husband: the modern Gothic," *Journal of Popular Culture* 6 (1973), pp. 666-691.

3 Michel Foucault, *L'usage des plaisirs* (Paris, Gallimard, 1984; volume II of *L'histoire de la sexualité*). Foucault's analysis of Greek and Roman sexual ethics has greatly influenced my thinking on the history of desire, although he would not necessarily have agreed with my use of his theory.

4 Psychoanalysis tends to assume that the baby is "normally" male; that is, normal development is often identified with male development while female development is explained by looking at how it is different from that of males. This means that psychoanalytic concepts have to be used cautiously and critically so as not to unwittingly reinforce sexism.

5 See Rosalind Coward, *Female Desire* (London, Granada, 1984), especially the section entitled "food Pornography."

6 See Cynthia Cockburn's study of gender and ethnic privilege in English male-dominated printing trades, *Brothers* (London, Pluto, 1982).ç

7 The key article in the feminist debate about women's visual pleasure is Laura Mulvey, "Visual Pleasure and Narrative Cinema," *Screen*, 16, no. 3 (Autumn 1975), pp. 6-18.
See also Teresa De Lauretis, *Alice Doesn't: Feminism, Semiotics, Cinema* (Bloomington, Indiana University Press, 1984) for further discussion.

CHAPTER SEVEN

1 Carol Gilligan, *In A Different Voice: Psychological Theory and Women's Development* (Cambridge, Harvard University Press, 1982).
In point of fact I disagree with much of what Gilligan says in this influential book. For one thing, I think her sample of girls is not ethnically and racially mixed enough, and therefore some of her conclusions probably apply mostly to white Protestant middle-class notions of femininity, rather than to women as women. Nevertheless, her critique of male bias in traditional ethical theory is a worthwhile one.

2 Adrienne Rich, "Women and Honor: Notes on Lying," in *On Lies, Secrets and Silence* (New York, London/Toronto, W.W. Norton & Co./George McLeod, 1979).

3 Mary Daly, *Pure Lust* (Boston, Beacon, 1984), p. xii.

4 Ibid., pp. 4-5.

5 Bell Hooks, *Feminist Theory: From Margin to Center* (Boston: South End, 1984).

6 Mary Daly, *Pure Lust*, p. 3.

7 Ibid., p. 68.

8 Ibid., p. xii.

9 Carole Vance, ed., *Pleasure and Danger: Exploring Women's Sexuality* (Boston and London, Routledge & Kegan Paul, 1984).

10 L. Weir and L. Casey, "Subversive Power in Sexuality," *Socialist Review* 75/76 (May-Aug. 1984), p. 154.

♦

−Liz Martin

MARIANA VALVERDE was born in Rome, grew up in Spain, and has lived in Canada since 1968. She has been active in feminist and other political activities in Toronto since 1976, and currently teaches women's studies at the University of Toronto.